Nautical Trivia Challenge

1000+ Questions & Answers

Volume One

by

Binnie Smith

Nautical Trivia Challenge
1000+ Questions & Answers
Volume One

by Binnie Smith

ISBN 10: 0-934523-89-4
ISBN 13: 978-0-934523-89-9

Editor@Middle-Coast-Publishing.com

How To Use This Book

Questions are organized in groups broken down into six different categories, namely:

RR Rules of the Road
PP Potpourri
RW Rivers and Waterways
SB Sailboats
TE Nautical Terminology
PB Powerboats

Answers appear two pages after the question.

For example, **Question Set 1** answers are found two pages later, on page 3 below **Question Set 3.**

Similarly, **Question Set 100** answers are found two pages later, below **Question Set 102.**

And so on.

In other words, in order to see the answer to a question, all one needs to do is flip forward one page in the book.

Question Set 1

RR Name the modern instrument that measures vertical and horizontal angles at sea: Sextant: secton; sextet; sexometer.

PP When a ship is afire and sinking rapidly, what should the Captain say to the Crew: Does anybody smoke? Where's the fire station? Abandon ship; I need one volunteer. . .

RW Waves tumbling on rocks, shoals, or reefs are called what?

SB A section of fabric in a sail is called a what?

TE True or False? The term crest refers to flood water's highest level.

PB Freshwater cooling refers to engine: Cooling; refrigeration; a tongue in check reference to sinking; air conditioning.

Answers appear two pages after their questions.

Answer Set 1. (See page 3.)

RR
PP
RW
SB
TE
PB

Question Set 2.

RR Speed and direction orders sent to the engine room are recorded in what book? Engine; log; bell; knot.

PP To propel a boat by working a bar from side to side is called? Sculling; scooting; yawing.

RW The Lake of the Ozarks is formed from the waters of which river? Osage; Ozark; Arkansas; Missouri.

SB Which of the following Japanese companies build outboard sail (auxiliary) motors? Suzuki; Yamaha; Nissan; Honda.

TE In the Navy, to have all night in means? You must stay on the boat all night; no night watches; twenty-four hour duty; twenty-four hour liberty.

PB True or False? Jetboats get better gas mileage than conventionally propped powerboats?

Answers appear two pages after their questions.

Answer Set 2. (See page 4.)

RR
PP
RW
SB
TE
PB

Question Set 3

RR A fathom equals how many feet in depth? 3 feet; 6 feet; 9 feet.

PP Name the famous steamship line that operated such vessels as The Britannia; The Lusitania; The Queen Mary.

RW A floating can or cask attached to ground anchors and used as a channel marker is called what?

SB The sail set on the aftermast of a yawl or ketch is properly known as the? Marconi; mizzen; main.

TE An Eskimo roll describes: A blubber and white bread sandwich; Whistling of arctic wind; Sailor's groan when they find they're boat is bound for Bering Sea; The method for righting kayak.

PB Thru-the-hub exhausts are limited to how many horsepowe? 300; 400; 500; 600.

Answer Set 1.

RR Sextant
PP Abandon Ship
RW Breakers
SB Panel
PB Engine cooling

Question Set 4

RR True or False? A stadimeter is an instrument for measuring the distance from an object.

PP True or False? Sea cows, also known as Manatees, a protected species in the US, make mighty fine eating.

RW How many islands make up the Azores? 19; 9; 12; 2.

SB The arch in a ship's deck that makes the center higher than the outsides is called what? Bulge; camber; side cut; bosun's peak.

TE Floating wreckage is called: Flotsam; jetsam; garbage; junk.

PB Volvo Penta's DuoProp propellers are modeled after? A Russian supersonic bomber; Resurrected steamship technology; Satellite positioning modules; Shark gills.

Answer Set 2.

RR Bell
PP Sculling
RW Osage
SB All four
TE No night watches
PB False

Question Set 5

RR A nautical mile, to a land mile, is about how many feet shorter or longer? 1200 feet shorter; 800 feet longer.

PP What well-known clipper ship is now famous as a brand of Scotch whiskey?

RW Sailors refer to the oceans and waters of the world as the what?

SB What color represents the port side of a boat?

TE When a shark on the end of a fish line is termed Green, that simply means the beast is: Worn-out; Still full of fight; suffering from *mal de mer*?

PB At wide open throttle gasoline engines burn about what percent of their HP rating, expressed in gallons.

Answer Set 3

RR 6 feet
PP Cunard Line
RW Buoy
SB Mizzen
TE Method for righting a capsized kayak
PB 300 HP

Question Set 6

RR The direction of an object from a boat is its?

PP How many stacks does the Queen Mary have? 2; 3; 4.

RW The Lake of the Ozarks if formed by what Dam?

SB Draft is which of the following? The efficiency with which a sailboat uses wind; depth of water needed to float a boat; Speed and direction of wind needed to fill the sails; Sideways slip of a boat due to water currents.

TE The Colecanthe is: A prehistoric fish; Jacques Cousteau Jr.'s new expedition boat; A rare breed of South Pacific Seagull; A sunken treasure ship (wreck) off Australia's Great Barrier Reef.

PB Who built the first steam-powered outboard motor? Eric Helm; Capt. MacKenzie Gerber, Kevin Randle; Wilbur Chapman.

Answer Set 4.

RR True
PP True
RW 9
SB Camber
TE Flotsam
PB Russian supersonic bomber (Tupelov 144).

Question Set 7

RR Name the nautical measure of speed, 15% greater than the miles-per-hour land speed measurement.

PP True or False? Sharks do not have skeletons.

RW A storm with winds from 32 to 62 miles per hours is called a what? Gale; blow; draft.

SB True or False? Port side of the boat is the left side.

TE The nautical slang name given to the Spirit of the Sea is what? Davey Jones; Captain Neptune; Captain Nemo; Dave Crockett.

PB True or False? The terms Jon boats and flat boats describe the same hull?

Answer Set 5

RR 800 feet longer (1.15/1)
PP Cutty Shark
RW Seven Seas
SB Red - Mneumonic: Port wine is red.
TE Full of fight
PB Ten-percent

Question Set 8

RR A boat not made fast to a dock or pier, and not underway, is said to be: Lonely; adrift, orphaned; afloat.

PP How many Americans died when the Lusitania sank? 135; 185; 128.

RW How long is the Lake of the Ozarks? 125 miles; 157 miles; 169 miles.

SB A twin-hulled boat is known as a what?

TE the term making knots refers to? Going fast; Securing a jib; tying off; Splicing hemp.

PB The most powerful production outboard motor is rated at how many horsepower: 275; 300; 400; 413.

Answer Set 6.

RR Bearing
PP Bagnel
RW Lake Bagnel
SB Depth of water needed to float a boat
TE Prehistoric fish
PB Wilbur Chapman

Question Set 9

RR There are 32 points in a complete circle around a boat. When sailing free with the wind aft, the term two points on the port quarter, describes which of the following: 22 ½ abaft the port beam; broad on the port quarter; 22 ½ forward of dead astern on the port side?

PP Name the weapon used to sink submerged submarines in World War I and II?

RW What is the term used to describe sea conditions that include 64 to 75 MPH? A gale; a blow; a storm; a typhoon.

SB Topsides on a boat is what? The bridge; the deck; the side from waterline to rail.

TE A Grinder: Sleeps with sailors for money; Cranks a sail's winch; describes a long storm at sea; means seasick and grinding your teeth?

PB True or False? When chartering a sportfish, never offer to take a turn at the helm because doing so offends the captain.

Answer Set 7.

RR Nautical MPH (knots)
PP True
RW Gale
SB True
TE Davey Jones
PB True

Question Set 10

RR The vertical distance from the waterline to gunwale is called what?

PP Dolphins are: Mammals; Fish; Arachnids; Reptiles?

RW Name the largest island off the Western coast of North America near British Columbia: Victoria Island; Island; Seal Island; Vancouver Island.

SB True or False? 12 meter yachts are so called because of their length.

TE To untangle anchor lines from one another is called: Clearhouse; birdnest; unmess the lines.

PB True or False? The Savannah was the first steamboat to cross the Atlantic Ocean.

Answer Set 8.

RR Adrift
PP 128
RW 125 miles
SB Catamaran
TE Going fast
PB 300 Horsepower

Question Set 11

RR One leg of the zig-zag course a sailboat steers in beating to the windward is: Broad reach; tack; yaw?

PP The naval rank just below Captain is? Commodore; Commander; Lieutenant; Lt. Commander.

RW Name the major Canadian seaport located 300 miles up the St. Lawrence River.

SB True or False? Modern day pirates still board ships and slash their victim's throats.

TE True or False? The term following seas describes the situation of a boat running with the wind.

PB Steam yachting was first introduced in America in what year? 1795; 1853; 1889; 1910.

Answer Set 9

RR 22-½ forward of dead astern on the port side
PP Depth Charge
RW A storm
SB The from waterline to rail
TE Cranks a sail's winch
PB False

Question Set 12

RR To name the 32 points of the compass in sequence is to?
Circle the compass; Call the compass; Box the compass.

PP Name the first European to discover what is now known
as San Francisco Bay: Sir Francis Drake; Christopher
Columbus; Giuseppe Veranzano; Lewis & Clark.

RW Name the bridge that spans San Francisco Bay.

SB The act of moving a vessel by means of a line or laid out
anchor is called what? Warp; Slide; Pull; Scull.

TE True or False? A *dhow* is an Arab sailing vessel.

PB True or False? A certain brand of outboard motor talks to
you?

Answer Set 10.

RR Free Board
PP Mammals
RW Vancouver Island
SB False
TE Clear House
PB True

Question Set 13

RR Name the term that describes to veer suddenly off course.

PP True or False? Canoes are considered to be exceptionally stable craft.

RW Name the seaport in Holland that handles over 25% of all seaborne goods in the European economic community.

SB A line used to hoist or lower a sail is called a what?

TE The sailor's name for a food stain on clothing is? Soiled Skivvies; Pusser's Medal; Galley Grime; Galley Gumbo.

PB The Carniti is an Italian diesel powered? Outboard motor; GenSet; Refrigeration system; Drydock.

Answer Set 11.

RR Tack
PP Commander
RW Quebec
SB True
TE True
PB 1853 by Robert Fulton

Question set 14.

RR How many compass points are there? 32; 36; 24.

PP True or False? Russian naval officers regularly compete in European powerboat racing competition.

RW The Lake of the Ozarks boasts how many miles of shoreline? 500; 700; 1100; 1300.

SB Sailboats get electrical current from: Solar panels; Wind generators; GenSets; Gennys.

TE The frayed end of a rope is called a what? Cowstail; Bird's nest; Switch end; Cat's cradle.

PB A ship going _____ is traveling faster than full speed but less than emergency full speed: Standard speed; Flank speed; Fast speed; Primary speed; Warp factor five.

Answer Set 12.

RR Box the compass
PP Sir Francis Drake
RW Golden Gate Bridge
SB Warp
TE True
PB True. Some Suzuki V-6 engines.

Question Set 15.

RR A large vessel with limited maneuverability would display which of the following: A warning flag; a day shape; a buoy.

PP True or False? The Midnight Express is the affectionate name give to a particular shark big enough to show up on the US Navy's SONAR at Guantanamo Bay, Cuba.

RW Name the chief U.S. seaport on the Pacific Coast. Seattle; San Francisco; Portland; San Diego.

SB Which of the following is another term for an anchor line? Set; rode; rig; chain.

TE Name the expression of surprise uttered when a ship strikes an object with such force that her ribs tremble.

PB As the legend goes, Ole Evinrude's motivation to build an outboard motor was due to: Ice cream melting; Insomnia; Laziness; A broken oar.

Answer Set 13.

RR Yaw
PP False
RW Rotter Dam.
SB Halyard
TE Pusser's Medal
PB Outboard motor

Question Set 16. ?

RR How many degrees are there between compass points? 11-¼ ; 12-¼, 15-¼; 18-¼.

PP What is the name of the ship on the TV series Love Boat?

RW Name the sea bordered by Denmark, Finland, Sweden, The U.S.S.R. and Poland: Caspian; Baltic; Red; Mediterranean.

SB In naval architecture, what does the acronym L.O.A. stand for?

TE A cutlass is what? A racing hull; Pirate's sword; Wounded female sailor.

PS Inflatable boats need a what? Otherwise they're hard to steer.

Answer Set 14.

RR 32
PP True
RW 1300
SB All four
TE Cowstail
PB Flank

Question Set 17.

RR Does the Greenwich Meridian serve as a base line of latitude or longitude?

PP During the Falklands War, A French Exocet missile sank her Majesty's ship the: Windsor; Sheffield; Ark Royal; Arizona.

RW Which U.S. vessel claimed to have been the first steamship to cross the Atlantic Ocean? Virginia; Savannah; Raleigh; Clermont.

SB When a sailboat is caught on a lee shore and has to work her way clear, she is? Clawing off; up a creek; standing by; abaft.

TE Self-contained underwater breathing apparatus is called gear.

PB The world's smallest production outboard motor weighs how many pounds: 12; 22; 14; 24.

Answer Set 15.

RR A day shape
PP True
RW San Francisco
SB Rode
TE Shiver my timbers
PB Ice cream melting

Question Set 18.

RR When the wind changes in a counter clockwise direction it is said to? Veer; About; Back; Sheer.

PP The line This was not a boating accident comes from which movie: Stakeout; Swamp Creatures; Jaws I; The Big Chill.

RW Name the island off the New England Coast that once served as a whaling center? Bikini; Nantucket; Shetland; New Foundland.

SB Which of the following is NOT a name for a sailboat keel? Bilge keel; fin keel; centerline ballast keel; loop keel.

TE To toss an item overboard is to it? Deep six; chum; shuck; torpedo.

PB True or False? Smugglers sometimes use 100MPH boats to transport bales of cocaine.

Answer Set 16.

RR 11¼
PP Pacific Princess
RW Baltic
SB Length overall
TE Pirate's sword
PB Keel

Question Set 19.

RR What do the initials IOR stand for?

PP This man was Secretary of the Navy at the outbreak of the Spanish-American War in 1898 and later became the nation's 26th President. Name him.

RW Name the stretch of water between England and France known to square-rigged sailors as the Sea of Sore Heads and Sore Throats.

SB A light line running down from the masthead to the boom on either side of the sail is called a what? Sail line; Mast line; Lazy jack; Boom jack.

TE *Mal de Mer* stands for: Seasickness; Dangerous waves; A storm at sea; Shipboard jinx.

PB True or False? Bent prop blades can wreck an engine.

Answer Set 17.

RR Longitude
PP Sheffield
RW Savannah
SB Clawing off
TE Scuba
PB 12-pounds

Question Set 20.

RR Name the light used to aid navigation that is smaller than a light station.

PP Full-grown Amazon River catfish are big enough to bite off: Your foot; A finger; An ear; A leg.

RW Name the island in the South Pacific known for its 600 ancient stone statues: Bikini; Easter; Jamaica; Bora Bora.

SB A short deck built across the back of a ship is known as a what? Aft deck; Poop deck; Main deck; Weather deck.

TE A _____ is an explosive device used against submarines?

PB True or False? Marine engines work harder than car engines.

Answer Set 18.

RR Back
PP Both Jaws I and Stakeout
RW Nantucket
SE Loop Keel
TE Deep six
PB False

Question Set 21.

RR True or False? International Offshore Rule is a method of predicting weather for navigation.

PP In what year was the Lighthouse Service transferred to the jurisdiction of the Coast Guard? 1952; 1918; 1939.

RW True or False? The passage around the north of Europe and Asia is called the Northeast Passage.

SB A sailboat changing direction by bringing her bow through the wind is called what? Nailing; Tacking; Screwing; Baling.

TE Loop charged refers to outboard motor: Exhaust and intake tuning; Electronic Fuel Injection; CD Ignition.

PB Two-cycle oil for outboards should be certified as what?

Answer Set 19.

RR International Offshore Rule
PP Theodore Roosevelt
RW English Channel
SB Lazy Jack
TE Seasickness
PB True

Question Set 22.

RR A bearing expressed in degrees relative to true north is called what?

PP True or False? Navy SEALS are fired from submarine torpedo tubes for stealthy infiltration of a target.

RW The Great Barrier Reef is located off the coast of? California; Florida; Australia; Hawaii.

SB True or False? The best boat shoes have cleats on the soles so you won't lose your footing.

TE True or False? A bumboat is used in ports to sell merchandise.

PB When a vessel travels over water instead of plowing through it, it is said to be what?

Answer Set 20.

RR Beacon
PP Your foot
RW Easter
SB Poop deck
TE Depth charge
PB True

Question Set 23.

RR The time, kept on a master atomic clock, that is used around the world by navigators in computing their position is known as what?

PP The Mississippi River excursion boat, The Delta Queen, had a sister ship named the . Delta Dawn; Delta King; Delta Lord; Delta Princess.

RW The passage around the north of Canada from the Atlantic to the Pacific is called the Northwest Passage, True or ?

SB An opening in the deck to provide access below is a Hole; door; hatch; portal.

TE A chopping gun: sprays fiberglass and bits of cloth; cuts fouled fishnets; cuts fouled fish line; is used to haul sails. ?

PB Propellers are most commonly made from: Copper; Aluminum; Sheet metal; Iron.

Answer Set 21.

RR False
PP 1939
RW True
SB Tacking
TE Exhaust/Intake tuning
PB BIA

Question Set 24.

RR A bearing expressed in degrees relative to magnetic north is called what? ?

PP True or False? Sylvester Stallone is a highly decorated Naval aviator from the Vietnam War?

RW Name the five oceans of the world?

SB A circular window in the side of a vessel is a what?

TE The first voyage of a completely finished and tested vessel is called its _____?

PB Stainless steel propellers are more efficient than aluminum because of their: Lower weight; Cupped leading edge; No flex profile.

Answer Set 22.

RR True bearing
PP True. under low pressure
RW Australia
SB False
TE True
PB Be on plane

Question Set 25

RR The lens through which the horizon is observed in a sextant is known as a what?

PP In what year was the Delta Queen launched? 1926; 1935; 1890.

RW The Panama Canal was more easily constructed because the oceans it connects lie at the same level. True or ?

SB Vertical partitions in a boat, corresponding to walls in a house, are called what? Bulkheads; sides; decks; beams.

TE The acronym WOT refers to an engine's what?

PB Engine oil both lubricates and _____ internal parts?

Answer Set 23

RR Greenwich Mean Time
PP Delta King
RW True
SB Hatch
TE Sprays fiberglass and bits of cloth
PB Aluminum

Question Set 26

RR To move, or to tend to move, a boat in a specific direction is what?

PP Who played the captain in the movie The Wackiest Ship in the Army? Richard Basehart; Cary Grant; Jack Lemmon; Ernie Kovaks.

RW The mass of coral known as the Great Barrier Reef is approximately how many miles long? 1000; 1250; 1500; 1750.

SB The officer in charge of the financial business of a ship is known as the what?

TE A large wave that rolls over onto a beach is called a: comber; reefer; roller; bowler.

PB Water injection reduces an engine's _____ requirement?

Answer Set 24

RR Magnetic Bearing
PP False
RW Atlantic, Pacific, Indian, Arctic, Antarctic
SB Porthole
TE Maiden Voyage
PB Cupped leading edge

Question Set 27

RR The International Offshore Rule is a formula for measuring and handicapping ocean racing boats. True or ?

PP What was the name of the first steamboat to have a steam calliope aboard?

RW Gale-force winds vary from: 10-27 knots; 28-47 knots; 48-63 knots; over 64 knots.

SB A line used at the bow of a small boat for towing or making fast is called a what? Painter; anchor; spring line.

TE The acronym PFD stands for a: Life jacket; A piston assembly; Bilge pump; a Coral reef.

PB Laying-up an engine refers to: Storing it for the winter; Commissioning it in spring; Rebuilding it; Replacing it entirely.

Answer Set 25

RR Horizon glass
PP 1926
RW they are not the same level
SB Bulkheads
TE RPM
PB Cools

Question Set 28

RR Name an instrument used in celestial navigation to calculate latitude and longitude. Sextant; Octant; Quintant; Quadrant; all of the above.

PP Mississippi River steamboat captains left bags of gold coins tied what onshore in return for firewood.

RW A relatively straight stretch of navigable river is called a what?. Narrows; reach; channel; straight.

SB The term for the different arrangements of sails and masts is what?
TE A sailor said to have swallowed the anchor is what? Ill with a stomach ache; retired; hiding something; in charge of the anchor.

PB True or False? Steam power is inherently more efficient than either Diesel or Otto engines.

Answer Set 26

RR Bear
PP Jack Lemmon
RW 1250
SB Purser
TE Comber
PB Octane

Question Set 29

RR The point at which a line drawn from the center of the earth through a boat would intersect the celestial sphere is the: Zenith; Greenwich Hour Angle; Parallax?

PP What was the famous message sent by Admiral Nelson to the British Fleet just prior to the Battle of Trafalgar in 1805? We have not yet begun to fight; England; England expects that every man will do his duty; Damn the torpedoes full speed ahead; Good luck, laddies.

RW To be classified a storm, winds must vary in force from: 10-27 knots; 28-47 knots; 48-63 knots; over 64 knots.

SB The major longitudinal member of a hull is called a: Sail; keel; shrinner; shiv?

TE True or False? A gob hat is a white sailor's cap?

PB Four stroke outboard motors fire how many times every revolution of the crankshaft?

Answer Set 27

RR True
PP Unicorn
RW 28-47 knots
SB Painter
TE Life jacket
PB Storing it for the winter

Question Set 30

RR A "Class B Fire" includes all but which of the following? Gasoline; kerosene; wood.

PP True or False? In 1915 Germany began a submarine blockade of Great Britain.

RW The _____ ? Current is a branch of the Aleutian Current and flows counter-clockwise: Florida; Alaska; Maine?

SB A ladder made of rope or chain with wood rugs is called what? A Jacobs Ladder; Daisy Chain; Larry's Ladder, Tar's Ladder.

TE Gel coat is the outer lay of a boat: Fiberglass, or wood?
PB Typically propellers turn? Clockwise; Counter-clockwise; counter rotate.

Answer Set 28

RR All of the above
PP Trees
RW Reach
SB Rig
TE Retired
PB False

Question Set 31

RR Athwart ships means: Across the boat; to turn to port or starboard; forward of amidships.

PP True or False? A petty officer 2nd Class in the Navy is the equivalent of a sergeant in the Army.

RW Hurricane-force winds vary in force from 10-27 knots; 28-47 knots; 48-63 knots; over 64 knots.

SB True or False? The mainsail is the principal sail on a sailing vessel?

TE Blow-out refers to: Blown head gasket; A cavitating propeller; Engine backfire?

PB True or False? Spark plugs are the most trouble-free component of the diesel engine.

Answer Set 29

RR Zenith
PP England expects that every man will do his duty
RW 48-63 knots
SB Keel
TE True
PB Other

Question Set 32

RR Name the device used for locating underwater objects by measuring the time taken for an electric impulse or return.

PP Another name for a captain or master, used mostly on smaller vessels, is

RR When a large wave fills a vessel with water, but doesn't sink it, it is said to.

SB Give the nautical term meaning "tight"?

TE A spoil bank is: a man-made island; Lloyds of London type insurance company; Food rotting in ship's hold?

PB Power-trim adjusts: Carburetor mixture; The propeller's angle in the water; Propeller pitch; All of the above?

Answer Set 30

RR Wood
PP True
RW Florida
SB Jacob's Ladder
TE Fiberglass
PB Clockwise

Question Set 33

RR Abaft means: The lowest point in the hull; toward the rear of the boat, aft of amidships.

PP In most pirate literature, Spanish coins were referred to as what?

RW Any deep, well-marked waterway in a shallower area of a lake, river, etc. is called a what?

SB A triangular sail set by sailing vessels on the stays of the foremost is called a

TE A timber head is most commonly used to: Tie-off a barge; Be burned in order to heat a steamship's boiler; Avoided; Considered to be an aficionado of steam powered punts.

PB On a Volvo Duo Prop drive system the propellers are: Of different sizes; The same size; Mounted on a single shaft; All of the above?

Answer Set 31

RR Across the boat
PP True RW Over 64 knots
SB True
TE A cavitating propeller
PB False

Question Set 34

RR What does Loran stand for?

PP Which state boasts the most registered boat Michigan; California; Florida; Texas?

RW The heaving or up and down motion of the sea came by the wind is referred to as ?

SB A lateral support for a mast is a

TE Give the term used to describe non-boaters by he

PB Worn rod bearings can cause an engine to -?

Answer Set 32

RR SONAR
PP Skipper
RW Swamp it
SB Taut
TE Man-made island
PB Propeller angle

Question Set 35

RR Astern means: The rear of the boat; behind the boat aft of amidships.

PP Admiral Russell R. Waesche was Commandant of the Coast Guard when? WWI; WWII; Civil War; Vietnam War.

RW The second largest river by volume in the United States is the? Missouri; St. Lawrence; Columbia.

SB True or False? Nuclear submarines have sails.

TE The Eskimo word for light is also the name of a canoe type craft used for fishing. What is it?

PB Evinrude and outboard motors, other than paint job and decals are exactly the same motor. True or ?

Answer Set 33

RR Toward the rear of the boat
PP Pieces of eight
RW Channel
SB Jib
TE Tie•off a barge
PB Different sizes

Question Set 36

RR The acronym SONAR stands for what?

PP True or False? Wing dams are natural underwater obstacles.

RW The rise and fall of the sea as a result of the gravitational pull of the sun and the moon is called what?

SB Any device used to reduce rolling a vessel from side to side is called a what?

TE A sudden violent gust of wind is known as a what?

PB The first production stern drive was introduced by which company in 1959?

Answer Set 34

RR Long range navigation
PP Michigan
RW Swells
SB Shroud
TE Landlubber
PB Burn oil

Question Set 37

RR Belay is to: Secure a line; secure a boat on solid ground; anchor.

PP The Revenue Marine was re-named the United States Coast Guard in what year? 1915; 1902; 1809.

RW Name the five oceans of the world.

SB The term bareboat refers to purchasing a boat with no extras such as ropes, anchors or instruments. True or ?

TE True or False? Cavel is another term for a cleat-like hardware fitting.

PB True or False? Diesel engines are built with sturdier components than Otto engines.

Answer Set 35

RR Behind the boat
PP World War II
RW Columbia
SB True
TE Kayak
PB Johnson

Question Set 38

RR What does the acronym RADAR stand for?

PP The Sea of Cortez salt content is what than in the Pacific Ocean?

RW True or False? Inland seas, such as the Mediterranean, are tideless.

SP True or False? The thumb knot is an excellent nautical knot.

TE The "Sun over the yardarm" is a nautical expression for? Time to get up; first watch on a ship; time for the first drink or the day; lunch time.

PB True or False? Outboard motors pose a more serious fire and explosion hazard than inboard engines.

Answer Set 36

RR Sound Navigation and Ranging
PP False
RW The tide
SB Stabilizer
TE Squall
PB Volvo

Question Set 39

RR When you give another boat plenty of room you give it a "wide?

PP This former Secretary of the Treasury was the founder of the Revenue Marine, which later became the U.S. Coast Guard. Name him. James Polk; Aaron Burr; Alexander Hamilton; John Paul Jones.

RW The St. Lawrence River is a tributary of which of the Great Lakes?

SB The side on a sailboat carrying her boom is the windward side, True or ?

TE The helm is where: You steer; You sleep; Talk on the radio?

PB Counter-rotating propellers result in a boat tracking: Neutral; To port; To Starboard; None of these.

Answer Set 37

RR Secure a line
PP 1915
RW Atlantic, Pacific, Indian, Arctic, Antarctic
SB False
TE True
PB True

Question Set 40

RR Lights required to be used by vessels at night are called what?

PP Name the Roman god of the sea.

RW The historic Hudson River starts as a trout stream from what lake in the Adirondacks? Lake Troy; Lake Marcy; Lake Tear; Lake Cloud.

SB All ropes and lines in and on a ship, which control a support sails, masts, and spars are called what?

TE The acronym TBT stands for a kind of what: Bottom paint; Distress signal; Global positioning system; Drug smuggler; Smuggled drug.

PB True or False? Outboard motors are made out of aluminum because of this metal's high resistance to corrosion.

Answer Set 38

RR Radio direction and range
PP Higher
RW True
SB False
TE Time for the first drink of the day
PB False

Question Set 41

RR Name the term for traveling down the forward face of a wave to increase boat speed.

PP True or False? Tracking blackened motor oil onto a teak deck helps keep the wood lubricated.

RW How long is the Suez Canal? 100 miles; 50 miles; 175 miles; 300 miles.

SB Fastening together two rope ends to extend the length of a line is called what? Hitching; extension; berd; rode.

TE Give the term for carrying a boat or goods overland around stream obstructions or between two waterways.

PB Magneto ignition is commonly installed on: Inboard Engines; The latest outboards; Older outboards; None of the aforementioned.

Answer Set 39

RR Berth
PP Alexander Hamilton
RW Lake Ontario
SB False
TE You steer
PB Neutral

Question Set 42

RR To determine the predicted height of the water at almost any time, or any place, one would refer to the what?

PP A famous mutiny occurred aboard the ship commanded by Captain Bligh. Name the ship.

RW How long is the Hudson River? 100 miles; 300 miles; 600 miles; 1000 miles.

SB True or False? The Loran was the first piece of electronic navigation gear that required little or no training in order to use.

TE The correct nautical term for what is commonly called a porthole is what? Scupper, scuttle, scar.

PB What element kills most lower units? Monofilament fish line; Submerged rocks; Saltwater corrosion; Bolts that vibrate loose.

Answer Set 40

RR Navigation Lights
PP Neptune
RW Lake Tear
SB Riggings
TE Bottom paint
PB False

Question Set 43

RR The forward most part of a bow is called as the what? Spear; stem; stern; spar.

PP The US battleship Maine blew-up in which harbor? Mexico City, Havana; Manilla; Pearl Harbor.

RW Chicago is located on the shore of which Great Lake?

SB Name Christopher Columbus' three ships.

TE Give the name for a small flat-bottomed, shallow-draft boat, that is squared at the bow and stern.

PB Name the compartment, located between decks on a large ship, used for treating illness or injury.

Answer Set 41

RR Surfing
PP False
RW 100 miles
SB Berd
TE Portage
PB Older outboards

Question Set 44

RR Vessels equipped with lights, fog signals and radio beacons are called what? Beaconships; beacon boats; lightships; signal ships.

PP Government Cut links which port with the Atlantic Ocean?

RW In what river in the Northeastern United States do both freshwater and saltwater fish live side by side?

SB Which of the following great men sailed the Atlantic Ocean alone in a six-foot long dingy? Sir Edmund Hilary; Sir Francis Chichester; Sir Coo Stark; Major Fogey.

TE A very strong seasonal wind that blows in Southeast Asia is called a what?

PB What company introduced the first 6 cylinder in-line outboard?

Answer Set 42

RR Tide Tables
PP H.M.S. Bounty
RW 300 miles
SB False
TE Scuttle
PB Monofilament fish line

Question Set 45

RR To steer a boat in the direction of the wind is? Windward; head up; broach; apparent wind.

PP True or False? The civil war ship The Monitor, is on display at the Smithsonian Institute in Washington D.C.?

RW Niagara Falls lies between which two of the Great Lakes?

SB A small shelter on the foremast for the lookout is called the what?

TE A log is a ship's journal but it also a means for measuring the rate of a ship's movement through the water. True or ?

PB Burning 110 octane aviation fuel in a marine engine rated at 87 octane will do what? Waste money; Burn a hole in the piston tops; Give more HP; Clog the carburetor.

Answer Set 43

RR Stem
PP Havana. Cuba
RW Michigan
SB Nina, Pinta, Santa Maria
TE Johnboat
PB Sick bay

Question Set 46

RR The light at Cape Hatteras flashes every how many seconds?10; 15; 25; 45.

PP Who played the Sea Captain in the 1953 movie "Fair Wind to Java" Cameron Mitchell; Fred MacMurray; Rory Calhoun; Tyrone Power.

RW What river region was the setting for Washington Irving's Rip Van Winkle and The Legend of Sleepy Hollow?

SB Some California 49ers got to the goldfields by sailing around: Cape Horn; Cape Fear; San Francisco Bay; Panama.

TE A Zerk fitting is the same thing as a what?

PB What company introduced the first 4 cylinder in-line outboard?

Answer Set 44

RR Lightships
PP Biscayne Bay
RW Hudson River
SB Sir Francis Chichester
TE Monsoon
PB Mercury

Question Set 47

RR The term to alter a boat's course through the eye of the wind is what?

PP Malcom Forbe's Hudson River party boat is the what? Dowd; Feadship; Browar; Cigarette.

RW Name the shallowest of the five Great Lakes.

SB The overhanging section of the ship's stern is called a what? Butchie; fantail; bulkhead; beam.

TE Give the term for the act of joining together two ends of a line.
PB Sacrificial zincs corrosion.

Answer Set 45

RR Head up
PP False
RW Lakes Erie and Ontario
SB Crow's nest
TE True
PB Wastes money

Question Set 48

RR All numbers on buoys increase in a downstream direction. True or ?

PP Name the 1955 movie in which Sterling Hayden portrays a naval officer who continues to serve despite the handicap of an artificial limb: The Pride & The Passion; The Enemy Below; The Eternal Sea; The Extraordinary Seamen.

RW The last tourist-steamboat cruised the Hudson River in what year? 1881; 1925; 1949; 1971.

SB Radar reflectors help a sailboat stand out on a screen. True or ?

TE The acronym OHC stands for an engine equipped with what kind of technology?

PB Who manufactured the first 100 horsepower outboard motor?

Answer Set 46

RR 15
PP Fred MacMurray
RW Hudson River
SB Cape Horn
TE Grease fitting
PB Mercury

Question Set 49

RR One minute of latitude equals: One nautical mile; 1.7 nautical miles; 10 nautical miles?

PP Where was Christopher Columbus anchored on January 1, 1502: Limon Bay, Panama; Madrid, Spain; Negril Beach, Jamaica; Havana, Cuba?

RW Name the great ship canal that connects the Mediterranean with the Red Sea.

SB A narrow berth for a boat, at either a pier or a dock, is called a what?

TE Name the disease, caused by a deficiency of Vitamin C, that was very common among sailors of the 16th to 19th centuries?

PB True or False? Marine engines originally built to burn Regular gasoline need supplemental lubrication in order to keep their exhaust valves from burning?

Answer Set 47

RR Tack
PP Feadship
RW Lake Erie
SB Fantail
TE Splice
PB Reduce

Question Set 50

RR A buoy with a conical top is called a: Knight; nun; pin head; coner?

PP Vietnam's Red River flows into the: Mekong Delta; Gulf of Tonkin; South China Sea; Coral Sea?

RW The inter coastal waterway is approximately how long? 1000 miles; 3100 miles; 2500 miles.

SB What does the acronym L.W.L. stand for?

TE The nautical expression for the bottom of the sea is what?

PB True or False? Engine anti-freeze transfers heat from the engine more efficiently than plain water?

Answer Set 48

RR False
PP The Eternal Sea
RW 1971
SB True
TE Over Head Camshaft(s)
PB Mercury

Question Set 51

RR The point on the earth's surface, to which the needle of a magnetic compass points is called what?

PP True or False? While rowing, the act of raising the oars too high out of the water and then burying them too deeply in the water, is known as windmilling?

RW A what occurs when powerful tidal currents move rapidly through a narrow passage over an uneven bottom.

SB Who is credited with discovering the Pacific Ocean? Balboa; Pizarro; Coronado; Cepeda?

TE True or False: The term crew can sometimes refer to a team of eight men in a racing shell.

PB A raised platform affording unobstructed vision for steering and navigation is called a what? Flying wedge; flying bridge; crow's nest; butchie

Answer Set 49

RR One nautical mile
PP Limon Bay, Panama
RW Suez Canal
SB Slip TE Scurvy
PB True

Question Set 52

RR Red buoys have red reflectors and black buoys have .
White; green; orange.

PP What was the name of the submarine in the movie
Operation Petticoat? Sea Hawk; Sea Lion; Sea Tiger.

RW The Canary Islands are located in which Ocean. Atlantic;
Pacific; Indian.

SB True or False: A sloop is always longer than 30-feet.

TE A bunked boat trailer refers to: The surface the boat rests
on while under tow; a trailer that's typically submerged in order
to get its boat out of the water, Both of the above.

PB The first 4-cylinder outboard was manufactured in what
year? 1918; 1928; 1938.

Answer Set 50

RR Nun
PP Gulf of Tonkin
RW 3100 miles
SB Length at the waterline
TE Davey Jones Locker
PB False

Question Set 53

RR The International Dateline is: A dating service for sailors; the new hot line to Moscow; a line running mainly along the longitude of 180; a point mid-way between Europe and North America in the Atlantic.

PP True or False: Poisonous sea snakes inhabit both the Atlantic and Pacific Oceans.

RW Name two of the four rivers that make up the Ohio River Basin.

SB A metal fitting, on a deck or dock, used to belay lines is called a .

TE The rowing term for accidentally catching an oar blade so that it buries under water instead of lifting free, is Catch a crab; plow water; trolling; hanging up.

PB True or False: 312 degrees Fahrenheit is the optimal operating temperature for an internal combustion engine.

Answer Set 51

RR Magnetic Pole
PP True
RW Whirlpool
SB Balboa
TE True
PB Flying bridge

Question Set 54

RR White buoys mark: Dredging areas; fish net areas; anchorage areas.

PP True or False: The Continental Shelf is the name of the dance traditionally performed by graduating seniors at the Annapolis Naval Academy?

RW An indentation in a coastline that is wider than it is deep is called a?. Cay; bay; shouncl; cove.

SB Who salvaged the Spanish treasure galleon Atocha: Mel Fisher; Eddie Fisher; Warren Billy Smith; Peter Janssen.

TE The nautical term foul means: Something that smells bad; something not as it should be; To go aground.

PB How many tons was the French Lines Normandie? 59,000; 71,000; 80,000.

Answer Set 52

RR Green
PP Sea Tiger
RW Atlantic
SB False
TE Both
PB 1928

Question Set 55

RR What is the line which limits a person's view of the surface of the earth and the visible sky? Maginot Line; Horizon Line; Greenwich Line; Nightline.

PP The United State Coast Guard was originally known as the . State-Side Navy; Maritime Marine; Revenue Marine; Home Waters Fleet.

RW Name the river that runs through the Grand Canyon.

SB The widest part of a boat is its —. Beam; bulkhead; butchie; bitt.

TE True or False: Two outboard motors are called an Borgen mount

PB A hull's waterline length is usually than its overall length.

Answer Set 53

RR A line running mainly along the longitude of 180
PP False
RW Ohio, Tennessee, Allegheny, Cumberland
SB Cleat
TE Catch a crab
PB False

Question Set 56

RR Under the IALA-B system, all specific purpose buoys will be yellow with yellowlights. True or False?

PP Fort San Lorenzo was a pirates haven for: Sir Francis Drake; Morgan; Pierre La Fitte, Blackbeard.

RW A small inlet protected by high cliffs is a . Cay; bay; sound; cove.

SB The Atomic Four is a: Obsolete sail motor; America's Cup contender; Nuclear Power submarine; Force Four Gale.

TE The nautical term for getting married is . Hitched; tied; bent on a splice; gaffed.

PB The Normandie was launched in what year? 1932; 1942; 1952.

Answer Set 54

RR Anchorage areas
PP False
RW Bay
SB Mel Fisher
TE Something not as it should be
PB 80,000

Question Set 57

RR Name the unit of measurement used to indicate the depths of the sea.

PP Name the pirate commissioned as an English Captain by the Colonial Governor of Boston in 1696. Roger John Brownlow Keyes; Daniel Todd Patterson; William Kidd; Jean Lafitte.

RW Name four of the five U.S. Great Lakes.

SB The opposite side a sailboat is carrying her boom is —. Windward; leeward; port; starboard.

TE Sailors circumnavigating the globe often transit the canal.

PB Phase-separation describes: Water separating from gasoline; Ignition voltage at the instant a spark plug fires; Oil frothing in the sump; Technique for removing cylinder head gasket.

Answer Set 55

RR Horizon Line
PP Revenue Marine
RW Colorado River
SB Beam
TE False
PB Shorter

Question Set 58

RR Who determines which bodies of water fall under federal jurisdiction? The Coast Guard; Congress: Department of Transportation.

PP During the month of January, the Caribbean Sea is typically: Murky; Clear; Cold; Stormy.

RW A narrow inlet or channel that connects two large bodies of water is a . Cay; bay; sound; cove.

SB The famous author, Zane Grey, loved .

TE Blowing great guns and small arms is a sailor's expression for a bad storm at sea; True or ?

PB Name the first steamboat on the Rio Grande. Corvette; Florence; Taco Belle.

Answer Set 56

RR True
PP Sir Francis Drake and Morgan
RW Cove
SB Obsolete sail motor
TE Bent on a splice
PB 1932

Question Set 59

RR The term used when describing locations at right angles to the center line of a ship is .

PP Name the whale in Herman Melville's epic novel of the seat.

RW How many states does the Mississippi River border? (specifically, border, NOT pass through).

SB True or False? To sail with the wind on a boat's quarter means with the wind on either side of the bow.

TE A GenSet generates .

PB Deep cycle batteries are most often used to

Answer Set 57

RR Fathom
PP William Kidd
RW Ontario, Superior, Michigan, Erie, Huron
SB Windward
TE Panama
PB Water separating from gasoline

Question Set 60

RR What is the Morse Code signal for SOS?

PP True or False? All Mercury and Mariner outboard motors are identical under the cowling.

RW Name the island called "The Rock", located at the southern tip of Spain.

SB A short length of chain that connects the back end of the jibboom to the front end of the bowsprit is the Chain cable; crupper chain; jibboom chain.

TE If a sailor had a Grog Blossom, he would have a .Large drink; red nose; hangover.

PB True or False? Any downdraft carburetor automatically passes USCG regulations.

Answer Set 58

RR The Coast Guard
PP Clear
RW Sound
SB Sportfishing
TE True
PB Corvette

Question Set 61

RR A "Class C Fire" is which of the following? Gasoline fire; electrical fire; wood fire.

PP Where is Iron Bottom Bay: Covington, KY; Boston, MA; Guadalcanal; Tokyo,

RW A breakwater built to protect a harbor entrance or river mouth is called a .
SB Sail motors should be shifted into neutral when under sail so that the propeller may .

TE The list of sick men excused from duty in the Navy is called the list. Blight; Cinnacle; Sick Call; Rickets Roster.

PB The first nuclear merchant ship was launched in 1959. Name her: Savannah; Love Boat; United States; Norfolk.

Answer Set 59

RR Abeam
PP Moby Dick
RW 8
SB False
TE Electric current
PB Run VHF radios. trolling motors and depth finders

Question Set 62

RR A pivoted mount to keep an object level is called a .
Gimbal; swing; macy; gyro.

PP The late President John F. Kennedy served on what ship during World War II?

RW Where are the European Channel Islands located: England; France; Norway; Germany.

SB When a vessel's sails are without a wrinkle she is said to be "full and by" or .

TE The horizontal flow of water caused by wind, tide, rotation of the earth, or temperature is referred to as the what?

PB A tachometer measures an engine's what?

Answer Set 60

RR 3 dots, 3 dashes, 3 dots
PP False
RW Gibraltar
SB Crupper Chain
TE Red nose
PB True

Question Set 63

RR Name the punishment device consisting of nine lengths of rope, each with three knots tied in them, connected to a heavier rope handle.

PP Water is usually deepest on the bend of a-river.

RW Edgartown is located on which northeastern U.S. Coastal island?

SB Name the tool used by sail makers to flatten the seams of a sail after the canvas has been sewn.

TE A vessel found abandoned at sea is called Condemned; floundering; adrift; derelict.

PB Hovercraft _____ the surface of the water.

Answer Set 61

RR Electrical fire
PP Guadalcanal
RR Jetty
SB Feather
TE Binnacle
PB Savannah

Question Set 64

RR The term to alter a boat's course through the eye of the wind is

PP The two-hour periods of duty on ship between 1600- 1800 and 1800-2000 hours are referred to as

RW Nantucket is one of the Islands. Elizabeth; Black;Yankee; Gloucester.

SB True or False: Sailboards are limited to a speed of about 10-knots.

TE Some sailboats are built out of cement.

PB Pivoting metal plates used to influence the performance of a hull are called . Trim tabs; coasters; sea plates.

Answer Set 62

RR Gimbal
PP PT-109
RR England
SB Rap full
TE Current
PB RPM

Question Set 65

RR To "sway away on all top ropes" means: Climb to the topsail; swing across the deck on the end of a line; a man will go to great lengths.

PP The Soviet Union is bordered on its Southern boundaries by: The Black Sea; The Mediterranean; Jordan; All three of the aforementioned.

RW The St. Lawrence River is a tributary of which of the Great Lakes?

SB A boat with a two masted rig, the mainmast forward of the mizzenmast, is called a what? Cutter; schooner; ketch.

TE Name the magnetized stone used to construct compasses.

PB True or False: For maximum performance a propeller should be as deep in the water as possible.

Answer Set 62

RR Cat-O-Nine Tails
PP Inside
RW Martha's Vineyard
SB Rubber
TE Derelict
PB Skim

Question Set 66

RR A crosswise seat in an open boat is a . Plank; slatel thwart.

PP Name the sea explorer said to have discovered the coast of North America in 1000 A.D.

RW The British Naval Anchorage of Scapa Flow is located in the Islands. Shetland; Flakland; Orkney; Hawaiian.

SB True or False? A gunnel is a type of racing sail.

TE True or False? The term runner refers to a structural component of a hull.

PB Name the first merchant ship sunk by a German Submarine in World War I. Liberty; Dunraven; Glitra.

Answer Set 64

RR Tack
PP Dog watches
RW Yankee
SB False
TE Ferro
PB Trim tabs

Question Set 67

RR Sailor's slang for anything overdone is .

PP The wide-legged trousers worn by sailors during the 16th to 19th centuries were called . Monkey bottoms; bell bottoms; galligaskins.

RW Name the wall built at the entrance of a river or harbor for the purpose of protection from the sea.

SB The term for the condition of a sail no longer flapping from lack of wind, but beginning to fill with wind is Awake; asleep; avast; tacking.

TE True or False? The term back full means reverse engines.

PB True or False? Hulls equipped with Mercruiser Stern drives can be easily retrofitted with OMC Cobras.

Answer Set 65

RR A man will go to great lengths
PP The Black Sea
RW Lake Ontario
SB Ketch
TE Lodestone
PB False

Question Set 68

RR is the term for chartering a boat with no crew.

PP The Golden Gate Bridge, spanning San Francisco Bay, was completed in what year? 1937; 1946; 1925.

RW The Channel Islands are off the coast of what state?

SB True or False? A gaff is a spar.

TE A rode is: t he center of the channel; a member of the crew on a sailing ship; an anchor line.

PB True or False? Submarines are propelled by electric motors powered by batteries.

Answer Set 66

RR Thwart
PP Leif Ericsson
RW Orkney
SB
TE True
PB Glitra

Question Set 69

RR A day signal relies on: Flags; Lights; VHF radio.

PP What was the name of submarine in Jules Verne's Voyage to the Bottom of the Sea? Nautilus; Sea View; Neptune; Atlantis.

RW Name the device for transporting boats from one water level to another.

SB A Danforth anchor has wide: Flukes; Snyders; A single Jody; Burrs.

TE A triple-hulled boat is a what? .

PB A small lightweight motorboat with an open cockpit is called a what?

Answer Set 87

RR Admiralty Sweep
PP Galligaskins
RR Breakwater
SB Asleep
TE True
PB True

Question Set 70

RR A hurricane warning indicates winds in excess of: 74MPH; 64 knots.

PP Water strongly saturated with salt, used before refrigeration to preserve meats, was called what?

RW The water from rivers that join the tide and increase the current at that point is called?

SB A full rigged ship has: Two masts with yards and topsails; three masts of three parts square rigged and topsails; four masts and square rigged and topsails.

TE The depth a vessel extends below the waterline is called what?

PB True or False? A skeg is found on outboard motors.

Answer Set 68

RR Bareboat
PP 1937
RW California
SB True
TE An anchor line
PB True

Question Set 71

RR A black and white spar has numbers.

PP In the TV series Wackiest Ship in the Army, who played the role of Major Simon Butcher? Richard Basehart; Jack Warden; Gary Collins; Martin Balsam.

RW The Channel Islands consist of islands. 4;8;12;16.

SB A grooved wheel in a block, or in a masthead fitting, over which a rope runs is called a .

TE The area beneath the floorboards, inside the hull, is the

PB Always replace all the spark in your motor at the same time.

Answer Set 69

RR Flags
PP Sea View
RW Lock
SB Flukes
TE Trimaran
PB Runabout

Question Set 72

RR The right side of a boat, facing forward, is.

PP The star of the TV series The Baileys of Balboa was Paul Ford; Henry Ford; Paul Douglas; Paul Lynde.

RW Lake Pepin in Minnesota consists of how many square miles? 45; 90; 120; 200.

SB The threads that run across a panel of sailcloth are called: filling threads; weft; fill; All three.

TE True or False? The general pattern of ocean circulation is considered to be anticyclonic.

PB True or False? Larger tow boats have as many as 10 rudders.

Answer Set 70

RR Both
PP Brine
RW Freshes
SB Three masts with three parts, square-i4g0d,and topsails
TE Draft
PB True

Question Set 73

RR A binnacle is: A natural formation on the hull; the housing on a compass; a connection between anchor chain and rode.

PP The TV series "Harbourmaster" debuted on CBS in what year? 1957; 1961; 1963.

RW Chicago is located on the shore of which of the Great Lakes?

SB A name given for all lines and fittings that hold the bowsprit on a sailing vessel in place is Coupling; clew; clothing; bobstay.

TE Dry-sailed means: Taking a boat out of the water; Racing in calm seas.

PB True or False? For safety sake, .safety chains should be crossed under a trailer's tongue.

Answer Set 71

RR No
PP Jack Warden
RW 8
SB Sheave
TE Bilge
PB Plugs

Question Set 74

RR The nautical term for a faucet is . Tap; cock; screw; bobstay.

PP On the TV series "Convoy", Ben Foster was the Captain of the Freighter . Flagship; Savannah; America; North Sea.

RW The Illinois River takes its name from what Indian Tribe?

SB Of two boats of equal size, shape & sails, the lighter boat will be

TE True or False? Leeward and windward are interchangeable terms.

PB True or False? Larger tow boats may have as many as five decks.

Answer Set 72

RR Starboard
PP Paul Ford
RW 90
SB Threads all three
TE True
PB True

Question Set 75

RR The forward part of a boat is called the .

PP Who starred as Admiral Nelson on the TV series "Voyage to the Bottom of the Sea"?

RW Name the shallowest of the Great Lakes.

SB A rope sewn to the edge of a sail to strengthen it against tearing is called a . Boltrope; batten: baseline; bobstay.

TE True or False? Hypoid 90 is most commonly found in a gear case

PB True or False? An engine's RPM run too high, or too low, will result in performance gains and improved fuel economy.

Answer Set 73

RR The housing on a compass
PP 1957
RW Michigan
SB Clothing
TE Racing in calm seas
PB True

Question Set 76

RR The left side of a boat, facing forward, is known as what?.

PP Name the island on the TV series Gilligan's Island?

RW A small, low island in the Caribbean is called a what?

SB Backing the jib to port forces the bow to ddo what?

TE A thermostat is part of the _____ system.

PB Name the steamboat that made the first ocean voyage by a steam powered vessel in 1808. Clermont; Savannah; Phoenix; Comet.

Answer Set 74

RR Cock
PP Flagship
RW Illini
SB Faster
TE
PB True

Question Set 77

RR True or False? Cabin sole is another term for the floor of a ship's cabin.

PP Name the boat featured in the 1965 TV series "The Baileys of Balboa". Island Princess; Island Queen; Lady Day; Savannah.

RW The oldest man-made waterway in the inter coastal system is: Pine Island Cut; Waccamaw River Passage; Dismal Swamp Canal.

SB The weights carried for trim or stability are called

TE True or False? Apparent wind is always forward of true wind.

PB Deeply nicked propeller blades require: Sand blasting; Truing; Blade replacement and re balancing; New prop.

Answer Set 75

RR Bow
PP Richard Basehart
RW Lake Erie
SB Boltrope
TE True
PB False

Question Set 78

RR Give the term used to describe all of the equipment and gear used to anchor a ship.

PP What kind of ship was featured on the TV series The Wackiest Ship in the Army? Schooner; sloop; ketch.

RR Any deep, well marked waterway in a shallower area of a lake, river, etc., is called a what?

SB A wide boat has more than a narrow one.

TE Which of the following terms describe stability: Initial; Ultimate; Positive; None of the above.

PB The first British aircraft carrier was the . HMS Langley; HMS Furious; HMS George III.

Answer Set 76

RR Port
PP Not named - uncharted
RR Cay
SB Starboard
TE Cooling
PB Phoenix

Question Set 79

RR The width of a boat at its widest point is called .

PP The 1952 movie "The Crimson Pirate" starred Alan Ladd; Kirk Douglass; Burt Lancaster; Errol Flynn.

RW What occurs when powerful tidal currents move rapidly over an uneven bottom or through a narrow passage.

SB The bottom edge of a sail is called what?

TE To turn turtle means to: Try to outrun pirates; capsize rather unceremoniously; Turn into the wind; Move down to a slower boat.

PB The USCG capacity information plate details a hull's maximum: Horsepower; Number of person allowable on board; Total weight; All of the above.

Answer Set 77

RR True
PP Island Princess
RW Dismal Swamp Canal
SB Ballast
TE
PB New prop

Question Set 80

RR Name the instrument used as a lever to pull a boat through the water.

PP Name the cargo ship featured in the movie "Mr. Roberts". Relient; Reluctant; Relentless; Rendezvous.

RW Name the deepest lake in the United States. Lake Mead; Lake Powell; Lake Michigan; Crater Lake.

SB In racing, what is the favored end of the starting line

TE Plowing refers to the situation wherein a boat's: Stern squats low in the water;Bow digs into water; the well-trimmed hull rides on an even keel.

PB Steam yachting was introduced in America in what year? 1809; 1853; 1889; 1912.

Answer Set 78

RR Ground tackle
PP Schooner
RW Channel
SB Stability
TE All of the above
PB HMS Furious

Question Set 81

RR Name the term for a mooring area, and also a place to sleep on a boat.

PP Name the star of the TV series Sea Hunt.

RW A part of the inter coastal waterway, from Anelote Keys to Carrabelle in Florida is named the . Lonesome Leg; Wilderness Bend; Horseshoe Cut.

SB Full sails are for and not for speed.

TE True or False? Tilt describes a motors angle in relationship to the boat's transom.

PB The replaceable pin fixing the propeller to the outboard motor shaft.

Answer Set 79

RR Beam
PP Burt Lancaster
RW Whirlpool
SB Foot
TE Capsize
PB All of the above

Question Set 82

RR When cradling a boat, proper support must be given to the hull to prevent .

PP Who played the title role in the TV series "Mr. Roberts"? Terry Smith; Fess Parker; Darren McGavin; Roger Smith.

RW Crater Lake is located in what state? Wyoming; Montana; Utah; Oregon.

SB True or False? A current stick is dropped in the water near a fixed object in order to determine the direction and amount of current.

TE A centerboard is a type of: Seat; Keel; Rudder; Galley table.

PB Name the first steam yacht in America, owned by Commodore Vanderbilt.

Answer Set 80
RR Oar
PP Reluctant
RW Crater Lake
SB Upwind
TE Bow digs into water
PB 1853

Question Set 83

RR The direction opposite which the wind is blowing is leeward; True or ?

PP The role of McHale in the TV series McHale's Navy was played by which actor?

RW The inter coastal waterways start and end in what two states?

SB A cunningham increases tension.

TE True or False? It's redundant to say knots per hour.

PB An overhead sunshade used to shelter an open bridge is called a what? Bimini Top; Bahama Momma; Shelter Half; Satan's SunScreen.

Answer Set 81

RR Berth
PP Lloyd Bridges
RW Lonesome leg
SB Power
TE True
PB Shear pin

Question Set 84

RR A passageway, through which a ladder or stairs leads from the deck down to the cabins, is called what?

PP In the movie Mr. Roberts, what nickname was given to the cargo ship by the crew? The Tub; The Bucket; The Barnacle Queen.

RW The boundary waters in Minnesota consist of how many square miles. 1060; 1660; 1860.

SB True or False? A boat is legally tacking when running from head to wind to a close-hauled course if beating.

TE True or False? Brightwork is metal that is meant to be kept polished and not painted.

PB What steamship company owned the Empress of Ireland? United States Line; Canadian Pacific Steamships; Cunard Line; Matson Navigation Co.

Answer Set 82

RR Warping
PP Roger Smith
RW Oregon
SB True
TE Keel
PB North Star

Question Set 85

RR True or False? A contour line on a chart connects points of equal depth or elevation.

PP What actor played the role of Ensign Charles Parker in the TV series "McHale's Navy"?

RR St. Anthony Falls, the first lock on the Mississippi, has a lift of feet. 25; 49; 60; 72.

SB A type of paint applied to canvas sails to prolong the life of a sail is . Cutch; chum; cutty; sea putty.

TE A breast line is a mooring line that runs at an angle from a vessel's fore and aft line.

PB True or False? Current is named for the direction to which it flows.

Answer Set 83

RR False
PP Ernest Borgnine
RR New Jersey and Texas
SB Sail
TE True
PB Bimini Top

Question Set 86

RR A boat on her beam ends when she is: healed over 90 ;healed over 60 ; the waterline is up to the widest point of the boat.

PP Name the actor who starred in the movie "PT-109".

RW What river is called "The Father of Waters"?

SB True or False? Some small boats have no jibs.

TE True or False? Broken water describes an area of small waves and eddies in otherwise calm water.

PB Which of the following ships did not belong to the Cunard Line? Queen Elizabeth; Ivernia; Windsor Castle; Caronia.

Answer Set 84

RR Companionway
PP The bucket
RW 1660
SB True
TE True
PB Canadian Pacific Steamships

Question Set 87

RR Light Lists" are published by the . National Ocean Service ; U.S. Army Corps of Engineers; U.S. Coast Guard; National Oceanic and Atmospheric Administration .

PP What is Popeye the Sailor's favorite food?

RW What two rivers make up Minnesota's east border and Wisconsin's west border?

SB The of the rudder increases with the speed of the boat.

TE True or False? To furl means to unfold a flag or sail.

PB Which of the following was NOT a World War II British Aircraft Carrier? Illustrious; Eagle; Jervis Bay.

Answer Set 85

RR True
PP Tim Conway
RW 49 Feet
SB Cutch
TE 90 degrees
PB True

Question Set 88

RR Name the walkway that connects the decks at the aft and the bow.

PP Name the comedy team that starred in the movie "Saps at Sea". The Three Stooges; Laurel and Hardy; Martin and Lewis; the Marx Brothers.

RW Name the highest navigable stream in North America. Missouri River; Snake River; St. Joe River; Salmon River.

SB The is a stay supporting a mast from forward.

TE The height from a ship's side from waterline to main deck is called: Running clearance; Freeboard; Mizzle; Pizzle.

PB True or False? The Mauretania and Lusitania were sister ships.

Answer Set 86

RR Healed-over 90
PP Cliff Robertson
RW Mississippi
SB True
TE True
PB Windsor Castle

Question Set 89

RR To determine the times when tide currents change direction you should consult the .

PP The Bermuda Triangle vertices are Bermuda, Miami, and

RW True or False? The average cost for a lock and dam on the Mississippi River was $3,500,000.

513 A Flemish begins in the middle and works .

TE Floating wreckage or goods thrown overboard is called: Jetsam; Flotsam; Floating debris; Garbage.

PB Who manufactured the world's first 100 HP outboard motor?

Answer Set 87

RR US Coast Guard
PP Spinach
RR Mississippi and St. Croix
SB Reach
TE False
PB Jervis Bay

Question Set 90

RR True or False? When two sailboats, neither under power, approach one another, the vessel with the wind on her port side has the right of way.

PP The movie "The Old Man and the Sea" concerned a Mexican fisherman, true of ?

RW Give the name given to an area of shallow water at sea. Bank; shoal; bar; rill.

SB How many sails were carried by Admiral Nelson's ship, The HMS Victory? 100; 36; 28; 18.

TE To ease of a line gradually is to ease off .

PB Who manufactured the first 300 HP outboard motor.

Answer Set 88

RR Catwalk
PP Laurel and Hardy
RW St. Joe River
SB Forestay
TE Freeboard
PB False

Question Set 91

RR True or False? In the Lateral System of Aids to Navigation, nuns are odd numbered and cans are even numbered.

PP Name the aircraft carrier featured in the movie The Final Countdown. USS Enterprise; USS Langley; USS Minnow; USS Nimitz.

RW Where was water skiing invented? Lake Tahoe; Wisconsin Dells; Lake Pepin in Minnesota.

SB True or False? Winds are named after the direction from which it blows.

TE To heel means to .

PB What was the name of the only 5 cylinder radial outboard motor?

Answer Set 89

RR Tidal current tables
PP Puerto Rico
RW True
SB Outward
TE Flotsam
PB Mercury

Question Set 92

RR A power driven boat leaving a berth or dock must sound a warning signal of . One short blast; one prolonged blast; two short blasts.

PP Who starred as the fisherman in the movie "The Old Man and the Sea"?

RW A long narrow bank of silt that forms at the mouth of a river is a Bank; shoal; bar; reef.

SB True or False? A small lightweight sailboat with an open cockpit is called a runabout.

TE The man who steers the ship is called the .

PB Dual engines are recommended for running because of the added reliability.

Answer Set 90

RR
PP -Cuban
RR Bank
SB 36
TE Handsomely
PB OMC

Question Set 93

RR A red topped white buoy indicates a boat should pass to the South or west; north or east.

PP A tacking duel is common in 12 meter racing. True or ?.

RW Water skiing was invented in what year? 1902; 1922; 1939; 1899.

SB True or False? To haul means the same thing as to pull?

TE Goods that sink when thrown overboard are called .

PB Mercury outboards was founded in what year? 1918; 1928; 1938.

Answer Set 91

RR False
PP USS Nimitz
RW Lake Pepin
SB True
TE List over
PB Cross

Question Set 94

RR A vessel 12 meters feet or more in length must have A whistle; A whistle and a bell; A whistle, a bell, and a gong.

PP Name the star of the 1959 movie "John Paul Jones". Fess Parker; Gregory Peck; Robert Stack; Alan Ladd.

RW A low tidal range is called . Neap tide; spring tide;fall tide.

SB What is the name of the vessel that served as flagship for Christopher Columbus.

TE A clockwise shift is called a veering or _____ wind.

PB A worn-out, and stripped vessel unable to move under her own power is called a: Hulk; Hogan; Nancy; Sweet William.

Answer Set 92

RR One prolonged blast
PP Spencer Tracy
RW Bar
SB False
TE Helmsman
PB Offshore

Question Set 95

RR The international Alphabet Flag Echo indicates: Keep clear; disabled; altering course to port; altering course to starboard.

PP Name the star of the 1979 movie "The Final Countdown". Kirk Douglas; Charlton Heston; John Wayne; Robert Mitchum.

RR A barge can move a ton of freight miles for the same cost a train would charge for 66 miles and a truck 15 miles. 450; 330; 210; 90.

SB A windshift while sailing close-hauled requires

TE True or False? Horse latitudes are those on outer margins of the trade winds.

PB The World War I troopship Leviathan was formerly a German Liner named the Vaterland; Deutchland; Berlin; Cologne.

Answer Set 93

RR South or West
PP True
RR 1922
SB True
TE Jetsam
PB 1938

Question Set 96

RR Vertical motion as the bow rises and falls is called .

PP Who played Nellie Forbush in the movie "South Pacific"?

RR What is the name given to a current's velocity?

SB The escutcheon of a vessel refers to her . Number of sails; name and home port; passenger list; cargo manifest.

TE True or False? A counterclockwise shift is called a backing wind.

PB True or False? Submerged outboard motors should be started soon after they are raised.

Answer Set 94

RR A whistle and a bell
PP ,Robert Stack
RR Neap tide
SB Santa Maria
TE Hauling
PB Hulk

Question Set 97

RR A white numerical pennant with a red dot indicates the number

PP The movie "The Man's Navy" starred which one of the following actors? Claude Rains; Henry Fonda; Wallace Beery; Charles Laughton.

RW True or False? A barge tow carries freight equivalent to 1000 railroad cars or 1500 trucks.

SB When the lee rail is buried under the water a sailboat: Goes fastest; slows down; Blankets; Furies.

TE A slot is the passageway between the jib and the: mast; mainsail; rudder; stanchion.

PB The World War I troopship Leviathan was nicknamed by the doughboys she transported. Big Bertha; The Big Train; The Floating Crap Game; The Europe Express.

Answer Set 95

RR Altering course to starboard
PP Kirk Douglas
RW 330
SB Course change
TE True
PB Vaterland

Question Set 98

RR Five or more short and rapid blasts on a whistle is the signal. All clear; danger; underway.

PP The movie Operation Petticoat starred Lieutenant Holden.

RW An area of water shallower than the water surrounding it is called a what? Shoal; eddy; neap; ripple.

SB True or False? The term island is another name for cockpit.

TE The term liberty ship describes a: WWII freighter; battleship; hospital ship; launch.

PB Which of the following aircraft carriers was NOT at the Battle of Guadalcanal? Yorktown; Saratoga; Wasp.

Answer Set 96

RR Pitching
PP Mitzi. Gaynor
RW Drift
SB Name and home port
TE True
PB True

Question Set 99

RR True or False? When proceeding downstream; black buoys must be kept to starboard.

PP Who starred as the Submarine Commander in the movie Torpedo Run?

RW The Inter coastal Waterways System was started in what year? 1875; 1905; 1928; 1949.

SB True or False? Just like an airplane wing, a sail too can Stall.

TE True or False? An Irish pennant is the dangling, loose end of a line of piece of bunting.

PB The French Liner Normandie was how many feet long? 859; 990; 1029; 1147.

Answer Set 97

RR One
PP Wallace Beery
RW True
SB Slows down
TE Mainsail
PB The big train

Question Set 100

RR A small light anchor for brief daytime stops when the boat will NOT be left unattended, is called a . Working anchor; brace; lunch hook; grapnel.

PP Name the star of the 1976 movie "Midway". Gregory Peck; Rock Hudson; Charlton Heston; Paul Newman.

RW A current flowing opposite of the main current is called an

SB A sail is considered trimmed properly when it is just about to: Luff; Ballon; Billow; Stall.

TE The Japanese word kamikaze literally translatedmeans: divine wind; suicide plane; dive bomber; Yank killer.

PB The Japanese Aircraft Carrier Unryu was sunk by the American Submarine in World War II. SailfIsh; Redfish; Swordfish; Bluefish.

Answer Set 98

RR Danger
PP Tony Curtis
RR Shoal
SB False
TE Freighter
PB Yorktown

Question Set 101

RR Numbers on waterway navigation markers increase in upstream or downstream direction?

PP The movie "Submarine Command" starred ^ as the Sub's Commander.

RW The Intercoastal Waterways System was completed in what year?1905; 1928; 1949; 1962.

SB True or False? The same principles of airflow that allow airplanes to fly helps sailboats move through the water.

TE The topmost end of a gaff is called a: Winnow; Peak; Apex; None of these.

PB The Queen Elizabeth was launched in what year?1938; 1930; 1946; 1929.

Answer Set 99

RR, True
PP Glenn Ford
RW 1905
SB True
TE True
PB 1029

Question Set 102

RR The end of a line made fast when the line has been paid out is called the what? Stump; bight; bitter end.

PP Van Johnson and Walter Pidgeon starred in the 1954 movie about an American Aircraft Carrier and her crew.Merrily We Go To Hell; Men of the Fighting Lady; Return of the Fighting Lady; The Lady Wins the War.

RW The Cape of Good Hope was discovered by early sea explorer? Vasco Da Gama; Bartholomew Dias; Prince Henry the Navigator.

SB Who won the 1927 race from Australia to Ireland, between the Hougomont and the Archibald Russel?

TE True or False? A pelorus is a navigational instrument used in taking bearings.

PB True or False? Pigstick is a detrimental term referring to outboard motors.

Answer Set 100

RR Lunch hook
PP Charlton Heston
RW Eddy
SB Luff
TE Divine wind
PB Redfish

Question Set 103

RR If a mooring buoy constitutes an obstruction at night, it shows as a: Steady light; slow flashing light; quick flashing light.

PP Which of the following actors starred in the movie SOS Titanic? James Farentino; Robert Wagner; David Janssen; Doug McClure.

RR The intercoastal waterways is approximately how many miles long? 200; 2600; 3100; 4000.

SB True or False? If a lowered sail is blown overboard a gust of wind could: Break the mast; Tear loose the sail; Capsize the boat; Part the lanyard.

TE The term scuttlebutt refers to: A container of drinking water; A rumor; Both of these.

PB The Italian Lines Flagship "Ref was sunk in 1944 by the . Germans; British; Americans; Russians.

Answer Set 101

RR Upstream
PP William Holden
RR 1949
SB True
TE Peak
PB 1938

Question Set 103

RR The terms kedge, stockless; Bruce, and plow refer to what/

PP The Battle of the Eastern Solomons took place when?
1942; 1943; 1944.

RW Name the islands that served as home for the 18th century pirate Henry Jennings: Virgin Islands; Bahama Islands; Bermuda Islands.

SB A sewerman works below deck. True or ?

TE Two-blocked means two have been drawn together as closely as possible.

PB True or False? Doubling horsepower nearly always doubles speed.

Answer Set 102

RR Bitter end
PP Men of the Fighting Lady
RW Barthalomew Dias
SB Hougomont
TE True
PB False

Question Set 105

RR An echo sound is used to measure what? Distance between ship and shore; depth of the water; accuracy of radar readings.

PP The British Naval hero Admiral Nelson was killed in what famous battle? Battle of the Nile; Trafalgar; Gibraltar; Battle of New Orleans.

RW Nantucket Island imeasures`` approximately how many miles long? 6;14; 40; 54.

SB Which of the following was NOT a World War II American submarine? Grayback; Trout; Walker; Archer Fish.

TE describes when a boat swings back and forth across its intended course.

PB True or False? Gasoline left in an outboard motor's carburetor during the winter never causes problems.

Answer Set 103

RR Quick flashing light
PP David Janssen
RW 3100
SB Capsize
TE Both of them
PB British

Question Set 106

RR The wheels or rollers of a block are . Sheaves; drums; shafts.

PP The name of the sea captain in "Treasure Island" was Long John Silver; Alexander Smollett; Fletcher Christian; Captain Queeg.

RW When the gravitational pull of the sun and the moon are at right angles to each other, tides occur. True or ?

SB True or False? The Flying Scud was a windjammer.

TE The term go into irons means you missed your: Tack; Mooring buoy; Slip; Station time.

PB Gearcases should be drained and refilled with fresh when laying-up an engine.

Answer Set 104

RR Anchors
PP 1942
RW Bahama Islands
SB True
TE Blocks of Tackle
PB False

Question Set 107

RR What were the original radio distress letters that were changed to SOS in 1908? C.Q.D.; M.D.M.D.; H.E.L.P.; D.A.S.

PP Edward Teach was the real name of the pirate known as . Long John Silver; Captain Kidd; Black Beard; Captain Hook.

RR The Missouri River was discovered by explorers in1673.

SB The only way to come to a dead stop in a sailboat is by into the wind.

TE True or False? A wayless boat is one without steerageway.

PB In World War H, a wolfpack of American submarines known as the what operated in the Pacific? Mickey Finns; Devil's Angels; Hirohito's Harlots; Death Fish.

Answer Set 105

RR Depth of the water
PP Trafalger
RR 14
SB Walker
TE Yaw
PB False

Question Set 108

RR A dog watch lasts for how many hours?

PP Alec Guiness starred in which 1962 movie about a Naval Commander facing opposition from his second in command? The Damned; Billy Budd"; Damn the Defiant; Mutiny on the Seas

RR When the gravitational pull of the sun and the moon are in the same direction or opposite each other, _____ tides occur.

SB Floating perfectly upright with no listing is called what?

TE A privileged _____ is the vessel with the right of way.

PB Who mandates and enforces engine room safety legislation.

Answer Set 106

RR Sheaves
PP Alexander Smollett
RR Neap
SB True
TE Tack
PB Gear oil

Question Set 109

RR The FCC requires boats equipped with radio transmitters to keep a log. True or ?

PP Who commanded the British Fleet at the Battle of Jutland? Sir Francis Drake; Admiral Nelson; Admiral Jacky Fisher; Admiral Jellicoe.

RW The St. Lawrence Seaway boasts how many sets of locks? 5; 7; 10; 15.

SB A number of tacks made to sail upwind is called a what?

TE True or False? The term hard alee is an abbreviation for the helm is hard to leeward.

PB The first commercially successful steamboat in the United States was the ____ ? Clermont; Savannah; Dixie Belle.

Answer Set 107

RR C.Q.D.
PP Black Beard
RR Marquette & Jolliet
SB Sheeting
TE True
PB Mickey Finns

Question Set 110

RR The most popular Marine radio telephone channels for

short range communications are on: CB; Ham; SSB; VHF/FM.
PP Name the sea cook in the book "Treasure Island". Long
John Silver; Silas McGinty; Archie Russell.

RW True or False? High atmospheric pressure tends to cause
water levels to rise.

SB The Windjammer sailed 449 miles in one day. Flying Scud;
Cutty Shark; Parsifal; Reliant.

TE True or False? A spark arrestor kills the ignition when you
turn off the key.

PB Fact: A pint of vaporized gasoline has the explosive force
of six stick of dynamite. True or False? A bilge pump mitigates
that hazard.

Answer Set 108

RR Two
PP Damn the Defiant
RW Spring tides
SB Even keel
TE Vessel
PB USCG

Question Set 111

RR Name the anchor used to get a boat off when she has run aground. Grapnel; kedge; spar; plow.

PP Name the Patron Saint of seamen.

RW The United States owns how many of the locks on the St. Lawrence Seaway?

SB The USS Constitution is better remembered as what?

TE Landfall refers to:

PB True or False? A pyrometer tells when an engine is losing compression.

Answer Set 109

RR True
PP Admiral Jellicoe
RW 7
SB Beat
TE True
PB Clermont

Question Set 112

RR Give the term meaning "to secure a line".

PP Such best selling novels of the sea as Jaws, The Island, and The Deep were written by whom?

RW The symmetrical curve of waves caused by the wind over large areas is called what?

SB True or False? Lifelines can be lines or metal pipe.

TE The term coming about is interchangeable with .

PB The Aircraft Carrier sunk in 1945 by a Japanese kamikaze plane was cristened what? Ommaney Bay; Manila Bay; Enterprise; Hornet.

Answer Set 110

RR VHF/FM
PP Long John Silver
RW
SB Flying scud
TE False
PB False

Question Set 113

RR A nun with a red topmost bad indicates that the preferred channel is to port or starboard?

PP Name the first European to sail around Africa to Asia. Vasco da Gama; Ferdinand Magellan; Marco Polo; Bartolorneu Dias.

RW Canada owns how many of the locks on the St. Lawrence Seaway?

SB True or False? It's impossible for a sailboat to sail directly upwind to a destination.

TE What do you call a knot worked into the end of a heaving line.

PB Name the ship used by Explorer-Oceanographer Jacques Cousteau.

Answer Set 111

RR Kedge
PP St. Elmo
RR Two
SB Old Ironsides
TE First sign of land after long sea voyage
PB False

Question Set 114

RR A space for stowage in a boat's stern is a? Locker; quarter; lazarette; cranny.

PP Who played the role of the crusty Sea Captain in the movie Jaws?

RW True or False? Tides are not affected by winds or topography.

SB The curve in the side or the foot of a sail is called what?

TE A nautical mile equals: 6080.2 feet; 6080 feet; 10000 feet; 1 Kilometer.

PB True or False? An outboard motor that burns a 100 to 1 oil ratio burns more oil than an engine burning a 50 to 1 ratio.

Answer Set 112

RR Make fast
PP Peter Benchley
RW Sine waves
SB True
TE Tack
PB Ommaney Bay

Question Set 115

RR In the new IALA-B System of Aids to Navigators, cans will be what color? Green; black; orange.

PP The first movie version of Mutiny on the Bounty was released in what year? 1939; 1935; 1943; 1931.

RW The Welland Canal in the Great Lakes has how many Locks? 6; 8; 10; 12.

SB The windward of anything is that which the wind hits

TE The helmsman of a ship's boat is called a? Cockswain; boatswain; stocker.

PB Outboard V8 engines have been around since when? The: 50's; 60's; 70's; 80's.

Answer Set 113

RR Port
PP Vasco da Gama
RW 5
SB True
TE Monkeys Fist
PB Calypso

Question Set 116

RR The color representing the starboard side of a boat is what?

PP Which one of the following was NOT an earlysteamship company? National Line; Allan Line; Kapler Line; White Star Line.

RW A what is a line of rock or coral, close to the water's surface, that could present a navigation hazard.

SB Sailing by the lee means the wind is hitting the side of the boat.

TE True or False? The term 'mast" sometimes refers to formalized proceedings commending naval officers.

PB Name the first steamboat on the Mississippi River? Zebulon Pike; New Orleans; Mississippi Belle; Clermont II

Answer Set 114

RR Lazarette
PP Robert Shaw
RW False
SB Roach
TE 6080.2
PB False

Question Set 117

RR The device that controls the rudder on a vessel is the
_____?

PP Name the actor who played the role of Captain Bligh in the
Oscar Award-winning version of Mutiny on the Bounty.

RR The Erie Canal was completed in what year? 1825; 1845;
1878.

SB A sail is aback when it is trimmed to windward. True or ?

TE The term not under command means: Its' been captured
by the enemy; It's disabled and uncontrollable; Its essentially a
derelict.

PB Marine engines use metal fuel lines because of their
resistance to what?

Answer Set 115

RR Green
PP 1935
RR 8
SE First
TE Cockswain
PB 80's

Question Set 118

RR Not all PFDs will turn an unconscious wearer's head upright.

PP True or False? Charlton Heston starred as Captain Ahab in the movie Moby Dick.

RW Do the tidal currents flow faster in deep or shallow water?

SB All of the equipment and decks extending above the hull are referred to as superstructure. True or ?

TE The term to cover and secure the hatches is referred to as what?

PB True or False? Rocky Aoki, the restaurateur, was nearly while killed racing powerboats.

Answer Set 116

RR Green
PP Kapler Line
RW Reef
SB Leeward
TE True
PB New Orleans

Question Set 119

RR The term high seas means: Rough water; seas north of the Equator; seas not controlled or claimed by any nation; extremely large, rolling waves.

PP The New York Yacht Club was formed in what year? 1914; 1919; 1844; 1886.

RW The three maritime provinces include New Brunswick,Prince Edward Island, and .what else?

SB A small enclosed space or cabin in a small boat is called a what?

TE True or False? A winch is a hoisting engine.

PB Name the arch over the cockpit that stretches from port to starboard.

Answer Set 117

RR Helm
PP Charles Laughton
RW 1825
SB True
TE Disabled and uncontrollable
PB Fire

Question Set 120

RR Give the term for a sleeping space or sailor's position in the ship's company. Rank; billet; slot.

PP The Japanese defeated the U.S. Navy in which one of the following battles? Savo Island; Betto Island; Midway; Okinawa.

RW The direction the current flows in called what/

SB True or False? The correct pronunciation for leeward is loo-ward.

TE A wherry is a: boat 12 to 14 feet long.

PB The first steamboat to travel all the way to St. Louis was the . New Orleans; Zebulon Pike; Effie Afton; Edmund Fitgzerald I.

Answer Set 118

RR True
PP -Gregory Peck
RW Deep
SB True
TE Batten down
PB True

Question Set 121

RR Name the instrument used to measure the precise angle a vessel is leaning.

PP Name the first woman to sail solo around the world.Dane Naomi James; Katie "Slip" Madigan; Rosalind Kelly; Maria del Ray.

RW The century-old resort of Bar Harbor is located on: The Bay of Fundy; Buzzard's Bay; Frenchman Bay.

SB A change of tacks is called a .what?

TE Name the winds of the tropics that blow towards the tropics, NE in the Northern Hemisphere and SE in the Southern Hemisphere.

PB Name the Japanese battleship, the largest ever built, that was sunk the U.S. aircraft on its first combat voyage.

Answer Set 119

RR Seas not controlled or claimed by any nation
PP 1844
RW Nova Scotia
SB Cuddy
TE True
PB Radar Arch

Question Set 122

RR A map of the sea is called a what?

PP In what year did the first steamboat travel to St.Louis?
1817; 1837; 1847; 1857.

RW An onshore wind creates much smaller waves than an off-shore wind. True or ?

SB True or False? You hoist or lower sails with halyards.

TE True or False? The term stand describes the condition when there is no vertical motion of the tide.

PB True or False? The transom is bolted to the stern post.

Answer Set 120

RR Billet
PP Savo Island
RW Set
SB True
TE Small pulling boat
PB Zebulon Pike

Question Set 123

RR A ladder of wooden rungs with rope sides is called a Jack Ladder; Parson's Slide; sailor's swing; stairway to heaven.

PP Yacht racing began in the 16th century in what Country?

RR The Great Salt Pond is located in: Florida; Massachusetts; Utah.

SB A projecting spar used to hold down and extend the foot of a sail is known as a what?

TE A taffrail log? Indicates boat speed; Burns without smoking; Is waterproof; Is used to repair broken spars.

PB True or False? Some propellers are made out of plastic.

Answer Set 121

RR Inclinometer
PP Diane Naomi James
RR Frenchman Bay
SB Jibe
TE Trades
PB Yamato

Question Set 124

RR If an overtaking vessel plans to pass on the port side of the vessel ahead, she must sound what signal? One short blast; two short blasts; five short blasts.

PP Jack Lemmon played the role of Ensign Pulver in the movie

RR Tidal currents may flow as fast as . 6 knots; 12 knots; 18 knots.

SB True or False? A turn towards the wind is called hardening up.

TE What is the term that describes when sails have been hauled in Close.

PB In the designation PT-Boat, what does the acronym PT stand for?

Answer Set 122

RR Chart
PP 1817
RR
SB True
TE True
PB True

Question Set 125

RR True or False? A ship's ornamented stem is called a prow.

PP Give the name of the ship featured on the CBS-TV series Harbourmaster: Luck Lady; Blue Chip II; Lady Belle; Harbor Princess.

RW Niagara Falls lies between which two of the Great Lakes?

SB A name given for all the lines and fittings that support the masts is what? Apparel; clothing; couplings; clew.

TE To do what to a sail means to pull it in?

PB True or False? Counter-rotating propellers help a boat track neutral.

Answer Set 123

RR Jack Ladder
PP Holland
RW Massachusetts
SB Boom
TE Indicate boat speed
PB True

Question Set 126

RR Name the instrument used to measure the depth of water by means of a timed sonic pulse.

PP On the Gale Storm TV show, actress Gale Storm played the Social Director on the which cruise ship? Ocean Queen; Island Queen; Island Princess.

RW Congress authorized a six-foot channel on the Upper Mississippi in what year? 1892; 1907; 1930.

SB True or False? Beam reaching means the wind is at right angles to the boat.

TE When a boat heels, it's doing what?

PB Standard day cargo barges measure: 100'x50'; 125'x25'; 195'x35'; 135'x35'.

Answer Set 124

RR Two short blasts
PP Mr. Roberts
RW 12 knots
SB True
TE Close hauled
PB Patrol Torpedo

Question Set 127

RR A vessel that has overturned is said to have what?

PP At the Battle of The Nile, who led the French forces against the British? Admiral Francois Paul de Brueys; Admiral Dumanoir LePelley; Admiral Rene Villeneuve.

RW Name the river known as The River of No Return? Snake River; Arkansas City; Salmon River; Colorado River.

SB A sideways leaning of a boat caused by the wind's force on the sails is called what?

TE True or False? A masthead fly indicates wind direction.

PB Two cycle outboard motors burn more than four cycle gasoline engines.

Answer Set 125

RR True
PP Blue Chip II
RW Lakes Erie and Ontario
SB Apparel
TE Trim
PB True

Question Set 128

RR A boat in your Danger Zone, from dead ahead to 2 points abaft the starboard beam, is usually the: Give way vessel; privileged vessel; burdened vessel.

PP Name the lap and foot covering used on a cruise ship while one is sitting on deck.

RW Which has the greatest gravitational effect on the tides, the sun or the moon?

SB Water deflected by the pushes the stern in one direction and the bow turns in the other.

TE The forward lower corner of a sail is called a what? .

PB True or False? Motor boating events have never been held in the Olympics.

Answer Set 126

RR Depth finder
PP Ocean Queen
RW 1907
SB True
TE Leaning
PB 195' x 35'

Question Set 129

RR Cardinal points and subcardinal points are found on a

PP The New York Yacht Club was founded by Commodore Vanderbilt: True or ?

RW Glen Canyon Dam on the Colorado River forms what Lake?

SB True or False? The tiller is abaft the mast.

TE The term abeam means at angles to the fore and aft centerline of the boat.

PB How many smoke stacks did the ocean liner Queen Elizabeth have? 2; 3; 4.

Answer Set 127

RR Capsized
PP Admiral Trancois Paul de Brueys
RW Salmon River
SB Heel
TE True
PB Oil

Question Set 130

RR When two power driven vessels are crossing, with a risk of collision, the vessel that has the other on her own starboard must give way. True or ?

PP Who played the psychotic captain in the 1955 movie Mr. Roberts?,

RW Tides normally cycle at an interval of hours. 6.2;12.4; 17.3.

SB Name the flagship of the French fleet at the Battle of the Nile. Orient; Conquerant; Orleans.

TE A backstay is used to support a(n): Engine Mount; Mast; Spar; Prop shaft.

PB True or False? The shorter a boat's scope the better.

Answer Set 128

RR Privileged vessel
PP Steamer Rug
RW Moon
SB Heel
TE Tack
PB **False**

Question Set 131

RR Name the cardinal points on a compass.

PP Name the world's largest man-made small boat harbor.

RW What is the largest dam in the world?

SB True or False? The term beam describes the maximum width of a vessel.

TE a heavy material like lead or iron, is placed in the bottom of some boats to give stability.

PB The Andrea Doria was owned by what shipline? Shaw Savil; Cunard Line; Italian Line; Appian Line.

Answer Set 129

RR Compass
PP False
RW Lake Powell
SB True
TE Right
PB 2

Question Set 132

RR When two vessels are approaching head on, or nearly head on, each should pass on the side of the other.

PP Who played the doctor in the 1955 movie "Mr. Roberts"? William Powell; Ward Bond; Fred MacMurray; Milburn Stone.

RW True or False? A breaking wave can haul as much as 12 tons of water at a velocity of up to 30 knots.

SB Name the Admiral Nelson's flagship at the Battle of? The Nile. Vanguard; Goliath; Orion; Viking.

TE Name the bottom part of the hull adjacent to the keeL?

PB A Danforth's dig into the bottom.

Answer Set 130

RR True
PP James Cagney
RW 12.4
SB Orient
TE Mast
PB False

Question Set 133

RR What was a Cat-O-Nine Tails and what was it used for?

PP Name the American aircraft carrier sunk at the Battle of Midway. Hornet; Enterprise; Yorktown.

RW Name the lake formed by the Grand Coulee Dam.

SB A rope tied from the end of the boom to point in front of the mast is a

TE True or False? A bend is the knot by which one rope is made fast to another.

PB True or False? A faulty thermostat can cause an engine to overheat.

Answer Set 131

RR North, South, East and West
PP Marina del Ray
RW Grand Coulee Dam
SB True
TE Ballast
PB Italian Line

Question Set 134

RR When two vessels are meeting, the largest vessel is required to sound the first whistle signal. True or ?

PP The character Captain Binghamton was featured on what Navy TV series.

RW A continuous oceanic wave pattern which follows the prevailing wind is called a

SB The lower, after corner of a sail; where the foot meets the leech, is a Batten; clew; hound; cringle?

TE Name the term for sailing to the windward: Beat; Reach; Run; Broach.

PB A battery's relative charge can be tested with a: Hydrometer; Potentiometer, Snyder sprocket; Diamphramis?

Answer Set 132

RR Port
PP William Powell
RW True
SB Vanguard
TE Bilge
PB Flukes

Question Set 135

RR True or False? A sailing vessel always has the right of way over a power vessel.

PP Name the boat featured on the TV series The Wackiest Ship in the Army: USS Eagle; USS Coco; USS KIWI; USS Hard Times.

RW The five Great Lakes cover how many square miles? 50,000; 95,000; 136,000.

SB To means to roll a sail snugly on a boom or yard.

TE The direction of one object from another is called a what?

PB How long was the German ship the Vaterland? 500 feet; 950-feet; 840-feet.

Answer Set 133

RR A whip for punishment
PP Yorktown
RW Lake Franklin D. Roosevelt
SB Foreguy
TE True
PB True

Question Set 136

RR Usually, vessels engaged in fishing have the right of way over sailing vessels. True or ?

PP Name the French Naval officer and yachtsman known for his many victories in single handed ocean racing, and for his book Lonely Victory. Eric Tabarly; Jean DuMois; Jacque Le Lane.

RW Which is the northern most of the Great Lakes?

SB A genoa is a large, overlapping jib introduced in a 6 meter race at

TE In a row boat, the footboard for bracing your feet is called a .

PB True or False? A cuddy is a decked shelter, smaller than a cabin.

Answer Set 134

RR Either may signal first
PP McHale's Navy
RW Swell
SB Clew
TE Beat
PB Hydrometer

Question Set 137

RR Give the term, meaning to "secure a line".

PP Name the girlfriend of Popeye the Sailor.

RW Wave that cannot be predicted with any mathematical precision are known as .
SB True or False? Mercator charts provide undistorted representations of the earth's surface

TE The depth of water a boat requires to float free of the bottom is called its

PB What was the name of the first steam ship built of iron: Aaron Manby; Constitution; Merrimac.

Answer Set 135

RR
PP USS Kiwi
RW 95,000
SB Furl
TE Bearing
PB 950-feet

Question Set 138

RR A chest, cupboard or small compartment for stowing
 gear is a

PP Name the riverboat in the TV series "Riverboat". River
Belle; Enterprise; River Queen; Gambler.

RR Oceanographers estimate that one out of every waves are
rogue waves. 20; 200; 2,000.

SB A sailboat said to be "full and by" is being held asclosely as
possible to the wind with here sails full and not shivering.
True or ?

TE True or False? The term scope refers to the length of an
anchor line.

PB What kind of a loose belt can keep a battery from charging?

Answer Set 136

RR True
PP Eric Tabarly
RR Lake Superior
SB Genoa, Italy
TE Streacher
PB True

Question Set 139

RR A fox on a vessel is a: three strand rope; an oar; a single strand rope; an attractive swabette.

PP The 1957 movie "Abandon Ship" starred: Tyrone Power; Fred MacMurray; Gig Young; Cary Grant?

RR What area is known as the Graveyard of the Atlantic? Cape Fear, North Carolina; Long Island,New York; Cape Hatteras, North Carolina; Cape Charles, Virginia

SB Give the term used to denote all of the various sails carried on a racing or cruising yacht.

TE True or False? A boom vang is typically found on Sailboats.

PB Anti-fouling paints are: Poisonous; Non-toxic; Alkaline; Acid.

Answer Set 137

RR Make fast
PP Olive Oyl
RR Rogue waves
SB
TE Draft
PB Aaron Manby

Question Set 140

RR If a vessel were to gripe it would: Turn into the wind; go to sea; return to port for repairs; take hold and go with the wind.

PP Name the friend of Popeye the sailor with an uncontrollable passion for hamburgers.

RW Name six of the states that border the Great Lakes.

SB True or False? Certain rudder fittings are called gudgeons and pintles?

TE When you throw a rope to another boat to make it fast alongside or to tow her, you are offering her a .Guest rope; mercy line; grop blossom.

PB True or False? Diesel engines weigh considerably less than Otto engines.

Answer Set 138

RR Locker
PP Enterprise
RW 20
SB True
TE True
PB Drive

Question Set 141

RR A ship's two largest anchors, carried on either side of the bow are called_.._,.

PP Which one of the following actors starred in the movie Across the Pacific". Clark Gable; Humphrey Bogart; John Wayne; Cary Grant.

RW The Gateway Arch in St. Louis is located on the banks of what river?

SB The larger the sailboat, the more support its must have.

TE The headstay, the backstay and the shrouds belong to the standing

PB In what year was the German liner Vaterland launched? 1913; 1915; 1917.

Answer Set 139

RR A single strand rope
PP Tyrone Power
RR Cape Hatteras, North Carolina
SB Wardrobe
TE True
PB Poisonous

Question Set 142

RR Give the nautical expression used when everything is in good order.

PP The 1951 movie The African Queen starred and

RR The system of inland waterway channels running along the Atlantic and Gulf coasts of the United States in the

SB A ball fits in to the slot on the boom to secure the boom

TE What is the name for a short line that ties a boat to a pier.

PB True or False? The British liner Queen Elizabeth saw duty as a troop ship in World War II.

Answer Set 140

RR Turn into the wind
PP Wimpy
RR Minnesota, Michigan, Illinois, Wisconsin, Indiana, Ohio, New York, Pennsylvania
SB True
TE Guest rope
PB False

Question Set 143

RR Give the term meaning excellent condition, derived from an important English seaport.

PP Who co-starred with Frank Sinatra in the 1945 movie Anchors Away?. Fred Astaire; Gene Kelly; Bob Hope; Bing Crosby.

RW The first steamboat traveled down the Ohio and Mississippi Rivers to New Orleans in what year? 1815; 1829; 1859; 1862.

SB A sailboat needs a ___ or ____ extending beneath the hull for stability.

TE True or False? Fairleads are eyelit fittings secured to the deck.

PB The American President Lines was originally known as what?

Answer Set 141

RR. Bower Anchors
PP Humphrey Bogart
RW Mississippi
SB Mast
TE Rigging
PB 1913

Question Set 144

RR A ship in fit condition to go safely to sea is said to be

PP Who starred as the submarine commander in the TV movie "Battle Of The Coral Sea? Errol Flynn; Cliff Robertson; Burt Reynolds; James Farentino.

RR In 1811, Robert Fulton's steamboat the Clermont traveled from New York City to Albany on what river?,
SB A nautical term for blocked is

TE A fid is a wooden

PB Outboard motors are mothballed what time of the year?

Answer Set 142

RR Shipshape
PP Humphrey Bogart and Lauren Becall
RR Inter coastal Waterways System
SB Vang
TE Painter
PB True

Question Set 145

RR The strengthening part of a boat's framework is the Crutch; camber; arch; apron.

PP Name the 1959 comedy movie starring Cary Grant and Tony Curtis featuring a pink submarine.

RW The steamboats Robert E. Lee and Natchez raced from New Orleans to where in 1870?

SB The LWL of a boat is .

TE A mooring line is fed through a .

PB True or False? Fogging oil is used to keep cylinders and piston rings from rusting.

Answer Set 143

RR Bristol
PP Gene Kelly
RW 1815
SB Keel, centerboard
TE True
PB The Dollar Steamship Co.

Question Set 146

RR A frame or latticework to ventilate a hatch is called a

PP Name the actor who played the riverboat pilot in the TV series "Riverboat". Darrin McGavin; Richard Boone; Gavin McLoed; Burt Reynolds.

RR Lake Superior is how many feet above sea level? 200; 600; 935; 950.

SB A strong timber going through the deck for securing lines is called a what?

TE True or False? The lower edge of a sail is its foot.

PB To cross a wake line smoothly, approach at an angle of about degrees.

Answer Set 144

RR Seaworthy
PP Cliff Robertson
RR Hudson
SB Stoaked
TE Marlin Spike
PB Fall or off season

Question Set 147

RR Give the nautical expression used to indicate that an order has been received.

PP Who starred in the 1959 movie Don't Give Up the Ship?

RW The canoeing area on the American side of the Minnesota-Ontario border, covering 1,660 square miles, is known as the .

SB Racing among deep water boats with a single rating is called what?

TE Current flows to the sea.

PB When underway, all powerboats throw a _____?

Answer Set 145

RR Apron
PP Operation Petticoat
RW St. Louis
SB Length at the waterline
TE Chock
PB True

Question Set 148

RR Which one of the following is a term describing the way an anchor cable enters the water: Astay; athwart; drag.

PP The movie African Queen" was set during which war?

RR True or False? The tidal atlas of any given area indicates the direction of the tidal stream.

SB True or False? A gudgeon is located at a sailboat's

TE Give the German name given to a tube attachment providing an air supply to a submarine at periscope depth.

PB True or False? Spark Plugs are easily broken.

Answer Set 146

RR Grating
PP Burt Reynolds
RR 600
SB Bitt
TE True
PB 45

Question Set 149

RR Give the nautical term for stop or cease. Astay; avast; amain; ahoy.

PP Who starred in the 1957 movie "Don't Go Near the Water"? Cary Grant; Glenn Ford; Bob Hope; Tony Curtis.

RW What island is located at Niagara Falls.

SB True or False? A head can be the top corner of a sail or a toilet.

TE Flood tide flows to

PB What was the tonnage of the German ship Vaterland, said to be the largest ship of her time? 13,500 tons; 54,282 tons; 43,392 tons.

Answer Set 147

RR Aye-Aye
PP Jerry Lewis
RW Boundary waters
SB Level racing
TE Ebb
PB Wake

Question Set 150

RR The opposite of being aboard is being .

PP In the movie "Down to the Sea in Ships" starring Richard Widmark; who played the captain of the whaling boat? Lionel Barrymore; Ward Bond; Broderick Crawford; Wallace Beery.

RW The boundary waters canoeing are is located in what State.

SB The was the first ship to have a mail plane take off from her deck.

TE True or False? To sail beyond an object is to overstand.

PB True or False? To luff, is to throttle down an engine.

Answer Set 148

RR Astay
PP World War I
RW True
SB True
TE Schnorkel
PB True

Question Set 151

RR A bow mooring line that leads aft to prevent the boat from moving astern is called a _. Springline; marlinespike; cast line; red line.

PP Name Popeye the Sailor's chief rival for the affection of Olive Oyl.

RW Who said "A river is more than an amenity, it is a treasure"? Mark Twain; Oliver Wendall Holmes; James Watt; Ralph Waldo Emerson.

SB True or False? To hike means to sail close to the wind.

TE The lowest class passage on the early ocean liners was: 3rd class; tourist; steerage; coach.

PB True or False? Small boats should face waves head-on.

Answer Set 149

RR Avast
PP Glenn Ford
RW Goat
SB True
TE Shore
PB 54,282 tons

151

Question Set 152

RR A line at the bow of a small boat for towing or making fast is called a

PP Who portrayed Admiral Halsey in the 1960 movie The Gallant Hours?

RW True or False? The Bermuda Islands are located in the North Atlantic only 670 miles from New York City.

SB The after edge of a sail is called the

TE True or False? The terms starboard and port are Interchangeable.

PB The French liner Normandie caught fire and sank in Sea; Bering Strait; Hudson River.

Answer Set 150

RR Ashore
PP Lionel Barrymore
RW Minnesota
SB Leviathan
TE True
PB False

Question Set 153

RR A cone-shaped canvas, held in shape by a metal hoop and used to reduce a boat's drift before the wind, is called a .

PP Who starred with Betty Hutton in the musical comedy Here Come Name the island in the Pacific that was the site of America's atom bomb testing.

SB Docking is best done from a angle.

TE A trough is the valley between .

PB Name the Japanese aircraft carrier sunk on her maiden voyage by the U.S. submarine Archerfish. Hint: Not the Shimano.

Answer Set 151

RR Springline
PP Bluth
RW Oliver Wendell Holmes
SB
TE Steerage
PB True

Question Set 154

RR A burdened vessel must give right of way to another vessel: True or ?

PP The 1941 movie In the Navy starred who: Bing Crosby and Bob Hope; The Marx Brothers; Abbott and Costello; The Village People.

RW Name the bay between Virginia and Maryland 195miles long and 30 miles wide at its broadest point.

SB Sailing any course, except to windward is called .

TE True or False? The term clutch dog refers to a particular part inside an Evinrude outboard motor's gear case.

PB The Bimini Top was originally used in the waters of the Islands.

Answer Set 152

RR Painter
PP James Cagney
RR True
SB Leech
TE
PB Hudson River

Question Set 155

RR True or False? To take a caulk means to sleep on deck.

PP Name the academy award-winning movie of 1953 set in Hawaii at the time of the attack on Pearl Harbor.

RW Cape Cod is an island off the southwest coast of Massachusetts. True of ?

SB The Coast and Geodetic Survey Offices are the principle source for: VHF radio frequencies; nautical charts; Boat Numbers; Maps of the waters.

TE are a shallow place in a river or sea.

PB The German ship Vaterland was captured by the U.S. in World War I and was converted into a troopship and renamed the what?

Answer Set 153

RR Sea Anchor
PP Bikini
RW Turkey
SB Shallow
TE Waves
PB Shinano

Question Set 156

RR A large ship designed to carry liquid cargoes is called a

PP Name the author of "From Here to Eternity". James Jones; Earnest Hemingway; John Steinbeck.

RW Cape Cod is a peninsula on the coast of Maine. True or ?

SB Tarred hemp or manila fibers used for caulking the seams of decks are known as

TE A high tide of 3-feet means the water will be 3 feet above what?

PB Tides, current and rough water will alter .

Answer Set 154

RR True
PP Abbott and Costello
RW Chesapeake Bay
SB Tacking
TE True
PB Bahama

Question Set 157

RR A sea running in different directions to a rapidly changing wind is called what?

PP Who starred in the 1961 movie Voyage to the Bottom of the Sea? Walter Pidgeon; Spencer Tracy; Victor Mature; Carl Thoresen

.

RR The Grand Banks are located off the coast of where?

SB Name the 18th century oar and sail-powered open boat used to transport troops.

TE The acronym VRO describes an automatic what?

PB Light scud clouds, alone in the sky, indicate what?

Answer Set 155

RR True
PP From Here to Eternity
RR A peninsula
SB Nautical charts
TE Shallows
PB Leviathan

Question Set 158

RR A term applied to the senior helmsman on a ship who takes over when she is entering or leaving a harbor is

PP True or False? Cary Grant starred as the crusty old salt in the movie comedy "Father Goose".

RW Name the large underwater plateau found at a depth of 600 feet off the coast of Newfoundland.

SB In what year did Ole Evinrude begin manufacturing his first outboard motors? 1910; 1915; 1920.

TE A burdened craft is the one without

PB The first outing in an unfamiliar boat should be in waters.

Answer Set 156

RR Tanker
PP James Jones
RW -Massachusetts
SE Oakum
TE Mean low
PB Speed

Question Set 159

RR A knot tied in a length of rope to prevent it from going through an eye is called a Square knot; sailor's knot; diamond knot_

PP Name the 1958 movie that starred Andy Griffith as a ship's cook.

RW What is the Gulf Steam? Any river that runs off into the Gulf; the Mississippi River; a large ocean current system; the marked boating channel in the Gulf of Mexico.

SB If you were in the fore cabin of a ship you would be in he Captain's cabin. True or ?

TE A Danforth is a(n): Racing sail; Anchor; Red channel marker; Brand of sail motor.

PB True or False? About 1,000 people a year drown as a result of boating accidents.

Answer Set 157

RR Cross Sea
PP Walter Pidgeon
RR Newfoundland
SB Actuaire
TE Oiler
PB Wind

Question Set 160

RR Red became the internationally recognized color for distress rockets in what year? 1854; 1917; 1954.

PP Name the 1979 movie about a modern day aircraft carrier caught in a time-warp and is transported back to attack on Pearl Harbor in 1941.

RW The group of islands called the Azores is located in the:North Atlantic; South Pacific; Mediterranean.

SB True or False? Battens fit into sail pockets.

TE True or False? The term "ironbound" was used to describe early warships built of iron.

PB True or False? Tugboats and towboats are in reality the same hull.

Answer Set 158

RR Quartermaster
PP True
RW The Grand Banks s r-
SB 1910
TE The right of way
PB Calm

Question Set 161

RR A gofer is a seamen's term for what?

PP Who starred with Francis the talking mule in the 1955 movie "Francis in the Navy"?

RW The ? Islands are located in the West Indies. Azores;Bahama; Solomon.

SB Name the type of boat with special fittings on her bottom to lift the hull out of the water at high speeds.

TE Pointing is a term that describes .

PB A motorboat in another's danger zone has .

Answer Set 159

RR Diamond knot
PP Onionhead
RR A large ocean current system
SB Falce
TE Anchor
PB True

Question Set 162

RR Gobbie is a British slang term for .

PP Which of the following actors did NOT appear in the
movie "From Here to Eternity"? Frank Sinatra; Burt Lancaster;
Robert Mitchum.

RR The Bahama Islands consist of 20 inhabited islands and
approximately how many uninhabited islands? 100; 200; 700.

SB The old saying "Still water runs deep" applies to: Current;
Depth of a keel; Thickheaded sailors; Walking the plank.

TE True or False? Composite construction describes a method
of wood planked hull building.

PB The first submarine to successfully destroy another ship
from beneath the water was invented by Robert Fulton. True
or ?

Answer Set 160

RR 1954
PP The Final Countdown
RR North Atlantic
SB True
TE False
PB False

Question Set 163

RR The tip of the arm of an anchor is called the

PP Name the actress who won an Oscar as best supporting actress in the movie "From Here to Eternity".

RW Barbados is a popular tourist spot located in the: ? Mediterranean; South Pacific; West Indies; East Indies.

SB True or False? When rounding a leeward mark, it's best to cut as close as possible on the near side.

TE The term hand lay-up refers to boat building.

PB Modern tow boats range in power from 3000 to 9000 HP. True or ?.

Answer Set 161

RR A non-alcholic drink

PP Donald O'Connor

RW Bahama

SB Hydrofoil

TE Sailing close to the wind

PB The right of way

Question Set 164

RR If you were foundering at sea you would be: Lost; ? capsized; drifting; sinking.

PP What was Captain Binghamton's nickname on the TV series McHale's Navy?,

RW True or False? A beam current pushes a boat to the tide at a rate equal to the current's velocity.

SB Auxiliary engine overheating is often caused by restrictions in the intake line.

TE The stuffing prevents water from leaking through the hull.

PB Most Mississippi River tow boats push their barges at a speed of 10-1/2 MPH downstream and 7 MPH upstream. True or False?

Answer Set 162

RR The Coast Guard
PP Robert Mitchum
RW 700
SB Current
TE False
PB False

Question Set 165

RR If you frap something you: Cook it; clean it; repair it; wrap it tightly

PP Lieutenant McHale commanded the PT boat on the TV series McHale's Navy. PT-73; PT-109; PT-66.

RW True or False? There are ocean tides on the Hudson River.

SB A rope sewn to the edge of a sail to strengthen it against tearing is called a ropestay. True or ?.

TE True or False? A skeg is a burst keg of rum. ?

PB True or False? GMC owned OMC.

Answer Set 163

RR Fluke
PP Donna Reed
RW West Indies
SB False
TE Fiberglass
PB True

Question Set 166

RR A tug boat with tow astern will show how many mast lights?

PP Name the actress who appeared in the 1948 movie "The Pirate". Lucille Ball; Judy Garland; June Allison; ? Doris Day.

RW The North Equatorial Current is anoth6r name for .

SB A strip of canvas laced across the bottom of a sail is called a ?.

TE True or False? Stern brackets are used to store extra sails.

PB Which marine engine manufacturer built Sea Drives.

Answer Set 164

RR Sinking
PP Old Lead Bottom
RW True
SB Cooling water
TE Box
PB True

Question Set 167

RR What masthead light pattern does a dredge show?

PP Name the actor who starred in the 1948 movie "The Pirate". Gene Kelly; Danny Kaye; Kirk Douglas; Ricardo Montalbon.

RW The ocean tides on the Hudson River raise the river level feet as far upstream as Troy, New York. 2-1/2; 4-1/2; 6-1/2.

SB Which of Columbus' three ships sank after hitting a coral reef?

TE Delamination describes separation of the layers of fiberglass and resin. True or ?.

PB True or False? Sunlight will deteriorate the gelcoat.

Answer Set 165

RR Wrap it tightly
PP PT-73
RW True
SB False
TE False
PB False

Question Set 168

RR The initials RDF stand for

PP Name the pirate nicknamed Calico Jack John Rackam; Charles Vane; William Bonney.

RW Name one of the two novels by Washington Irving based on the folklore of the Hudson River region.

SB The rudder pintels on a sailing vessel fit into a metal fitting known as a .

TE Electrolyis is a term for metal

PB Scratches or nicks in exterior gel coat should be filled with or

Answer Set 166

RR 3 white - one above the other
PP Judy Garland
RW The Gulf Stream
SB Bonnet
TE
PB OMC

Question Set 169

RR What does the abbreviation "Cr. stand for on a nautical chart?

PP Which of the following was NOT the name of a pirate? Bartholomew Roberts; Howell Davis; Charles Vane; Peter Pan.

RW When a current is "beam on", it is from the side of a vessel. True or ?.

SB The selection of is affected by engine HP, RPM, reduction gear, volume of hull and space available for the installation.

TE Electro galvanic corrosion is another word for what?

PB Name the world's first nuclear powered submarine.

Answer Set 167

RR Two red lights, one above the other
PP Gene Kelly
RR 4-½ feet
SB Santa Maria
TE True
PB True

Question Set 170

RR On a nautical chart, the abbreviation "Hr. stand for what?

PP Was it truth or myth that pirates made their captives walk the plank?

RW A relatively high tidal range, up to 10% higher than normal, is called what? Springtide; neap tide; fall tide; ebb tide.

SB Some sailboats used a two-bladed propeller for minimum drag.

TE True or False? A feathering propeller is one that has thin leading edges on its blades.

PB Name the sister ship of the World War II German battleship Bismark.

Answer Set 168

RR Radio direction finder
PP John Rackam
RW The Legend of Sleepy Hollow and Rip Van Winkle
SB Gudgeon
TE Corrosion
PB Epoxy glue, epoxy putty

Question Set 171

RR On a nautical chart the letter P abbreviation stands for what?

PP Name the pirate hanged in the year 1701, who was also a New York merchant.

RR If the tide tables show 9.5 feet, then that means the average level at high tide is 9.5 feet above the average level at low tide. True or False?

SB How many guns were carried by the 18th century fighting ships classed as first raters? 40 to 60; 60 to 80; 80 to 100; more than 100.

TE Deadrise describes the amount of Vee in a what?

PB Flat bottom hulls leave ? wakes.

Answer Set 169

RR Creek
PP Peter Pan
RR True
SB Propeller size
TE Electrolysis
PB Nautilus

Question Set 172

RR On a nautical chart the abbreviation "pass" stands for what?

PP Name the actor who won an Oscar for his performance in From Here to Eternity.

RW Name the large island in the West Indies known; for its cigars, Russian missiles and Carmen Miranda.

SB Motor boating events were held in the Olympic games for the only time in what year? 1908; 1912; 1916; 1920.

TE True or False? A chine is the intersection line of the bottom and hull sides.

PB Alcohol burns with a clearly _____ flame.

Answer Set 170

RR Harbor
PP Myth
RR Springtide
SB Folding propeller
TE False
PB Tirpitz

Question Set 173

RR What does the abbreviation "Linde" mean on a nautical chart?,

PP Name the actor who starred as Popeye the Sailor in the 1980 movie.

RR The Suez Canal opened in what year?, 1869; 1899; 1912; 1952.

SB Shear pins provide a line between the and the

TE True or False? A rub rail is the topmost cavel on a mast.

PB The open class Olympic motorboat gold medal was won by what nation? Great Britain; Australia; Germany; France.

Answer Set 171

RR Port
PP Captain William Kidd
RR True
SB Over 100
TE Hull
PB Small

Question Set 174

RR True or False? A radio direction-finder is a device used to find your favorite FM station.

PP True of ? John Wayne played a German merchant sea captain in the movies "Sea Chase".

RW A stretch of water enclosed or nearly enclosed by coral islands is called a ?.

SB How much black powder did Admiral Nelson's ship HMS Victory store on board? 1 ton; 15 tons; 35 tons.

TE A Henweigh is a: Mythological outboard motor company; Sailing ship passage with women aboard; Brass fixture; Copper fixture.

PB True or False? Some propeller's have rubber hubs.

Answer Set 172

RR Passages
PP Frank Sinatra
RW Cuba
SB 1908
TE True
PB Invisible

Question Set 175

RR A boat at anchor at night must display a light visible 32 points. Red; white; green.

PP Name the actress who starred in the movie Sea Devils. Yvonne DeCarlo; Lana Turner; Vanessa Redgrave; Natalie Wood.

RW Name four of the eight Channel Islands off the California coast.

SB Name the five masted German sailing ship of the early 1900's nicknamed Queen of the Seas.

TE True or False? The acronym EPIRB refers to an emergency position indicating radio beacon.

PB One of the chief advantages of a fiberglass is that it can be repaired by anyone with moderate skills and hand tools.

Answer Set 173

RR Landing place
PP Robin Williams
RW 1869
SB Propshaft. propeller
TE False
PB France

Question Set 176

No further questions

Answer Set 175

RR White
PP Yvonne DeCarlo
RW San Miguel, Ancapy, Santa Cruz, Santa Rosa,
SanClemente, Santa Catalina, San Nicholas, Santa Barbara
SB Intrepid
TE True
PB Hull

Question Set 177

No further questions.

Answer Set 174

RR False
PP True
RW Lagoon
SB 35 tons
TE Mythological outboard motor company
PB True

www.ingramcontent.com/pod-product-compliance
Lightning Source LLC
Chambersburg PA
CBHW071531040426

42452CB00008B/973